Tools for Continuing
Professional Development

Tools for Continuing
Professional Development

edited by
Chia Swee Hong and Deborah Harrison

Quay Books
MA Healthcare Limited

Quay Books Division, MA Healthcare Limited, Jesses Farm, Snow Hill, Dinton, Wiltshire SP3 5HN

British Library Cataloguing-in-Publication Data
A catalogue record is available for this book

© MA Healthcare Limited 2004
ISBN 1 85642 250 X

Printed in the UK by Cromwell Press, Trowbridge

Contents

List of contributors

Kim Atkinson was formerly Lecturer in Occupational Therapy, School of Allied Professions, University of East Anglia, Norwich NR4 7TJ

Gail Boniface is Senior Lecturer, Department of Occupational Therapy Education, School of Healthcare Studies, University of Wales College of Medicine, Cardiff CF14 4XN

Peter Burley is Director of Education and Policy, Health Professions Council, London SE11 4BU

Neil Gopee, is Senior Lecturer, School of Health and Social Sciences, Nursing and Midwifery, Coventry University, Coventry CV1 5FB

Deborah Harrison is Lecturer in Occupational Therapy, School of Allied Health Professions, University of East Anglia, Norwich NR4 7TJ

Chia Swee Hong is Lecturer, School of Allied Health Professionals, University of East Anglia, Norwich NR4 7TJ

Rod Lambert is Lecturer in Occupational Therapy, School of Allied Health Professionals, University of East Anglia, Norwich NR4 7TJ

Hilary Lawler was formerly Lecturer in Physiotherapy, School of Allied Health Professionals, University of East Anglia, Norwich NR4 7TJ

Maggie McArthur is Lecturer in Occupational Therapy, School of Allied Health Professionals, University of East Anglia, Norwich NR4 7TJ

Ann Moore is Director, Clinical Research Centre for Health Professions, University of Brighton, Eastbourne BN2 4AT

Emma Payne is Occupational Therapist, Therapy Services, Derbyshire Royal Infirmary, Derby DE1 2QY

Eve Pringle is Senior Lecturer in Occupational Therapy, Canterbury Christ Church University College, Canterbury, Kent CT1 1QU

Robin Shutt is Lecturer in Physiotherapy, School of Allied Health Professionals, University of East Anglia, Norwich NR4 7TJ

Nicola Spalding is Senior Lecturer in Occupational Therapy, School of Allied Health Professionals, University of East Anglia, Norwich NR4 7TJ

Richard Stephenson, is Senior Lecturer in Physiotherapy, School of Health, University of East Anglia, Norwich NR4 7TJ

Sandra Stewart, is Senior Lecturer, School of Allied Health Professionals, University of East Anglia, Norwich NR4 7TJ

Elizabeth Walker was formerly Lecturer in Physiotherapy, School of Allied Health Professionals, University of East Anglia, Norwich NR4 7TJ

Catherine Wells is Senior Lecturer in Occupational Therapy and Practice Placement Coordinator, School of Allied Health Professionals, University of East Anglia, Norwich NR4 7TJ

Preface

We were one of the first schools to have initiated education in continuing professional development (CPD). In 1997, a major conference was held at the school to introduce the concepts and tools of CPD to allied health professionals (AHPs). The conference attracted a large number of AHPs from a variety of settings. Many of the conference delegates asked for the proceedings from the presentations and workshops to be documented for future reference and the results were a series of articles published in the *International Journal of Therapy and Rehabilitation*. Some of the chapters in this book arose from these articles while others have been selected to provide a broader perspective of continuing professional development.

This book is published in a rapidly changing health and social care context. The legislation that regulates professional registration has changed in 2002 and has not, at the time of writing, been fully implemented. Many of the chapters include principles and tools that will have currency for a long time, however, some will have less currency as things evolve, but they encapsulate the situation as it stands. As this is a collection of published articles, in this changing context, some of the terminology will vary. Therefore, there are references to the Council for Professions Supplementary to Medicine, but as *Chapter 10* makes clear, the Health Professions Council has replaced this. Also, the term professions allied to medicine has been used, but is now superseded by allied health professionals and likewise, fieldwork placement is now called practice placement. The School of Occupational Therapy and Physiotherapy is now the School of Allied Health Professions.

We feel that this book will support the professional CPD packages that have been developed by the professional bodies.

Chia Swee Hong
Deborah Harrison
June 2004

Foreword

Effectively managing and developing high-quality clinical practice and addressing clinical governance needs require a culture of continuing professional development (CPD), which can explore whether what is being done is the right thing to meet the needs of the consumer, the commissioner and the health professionals providing the service. If the focus of activity is correct, it is also vital to establish if that focus is being achieved in the right way. This relies, in part, on a comprehensive understanding of what resources and strategies are required. It demands identification of professional development needs alongside implementation plans to set objectives, integrate training and evaluate outcomes. This needs to be addressed through sound educational principles, effective project and personnel management, a willingness to be both generator and critical consumer of evidence-based practice and a willingness to respond to the changing agenda.

In addition, CPD influences health professionals' evaluation of job satisfaction, especially as major motivational factors for job satisfaction are achievement, recognition, the actual work, responsibility, advancement and a belief in a successful outcome (Timmreck, 2001). Inability to respond to the challenges can produce negative factors of guilt, powerlessness and lacking control. Therefore, job satisfaction is an essential component of retaining and recruiting staff.

Culture change

To facilitate these activities there has to be a culture change that fully recognizes and protects time for CPD. The arrangement of this time allocation has to be considered creatively and with the needs of both the individual and the service taken into account. To facilitate this time away from direct clinical contact, there needs to be dedicated funding and a review of workload allocation to counteract the great difficulty with workload management.

Currently, there appears to be funding for CPD without the infrastructure to enable the money to be used to its best effect. This creates frustration among health professionals, severely reduces job satisfaction and so becomes counterproductive to the original aims of CPD. Key stakeholders have to work towards a more congruent understanding of the barriers to CPD between managers and the health professionals they manage.

Educational change

A way of addressing the considerable problems that some professionals are experiencing with trying to engage in meaningful and purposeful CPD activities would be to develop coordinated, facilitated and work-based activities that were valued, validated and protected. The reliance on the external expert has to be re-examined. An expert-led didactic approach has produced a reliance on giving information to course attendants who then struggle to make the theory/practice links and experience difficulties and frustrations in implementing changes within their work practices. A move towards a greater emphasis on reflective practice and self-directed learning will develop more independent learners. However, where it is appropriate to access expertise, it has been identified that there is difficulty in identifying relevant high-quality expertise. This is particularly pertinent when considering the effect of specific new initiatives, such as the move to primary care trusts, as the reallocation of health professionals into smaller, community-based units will have an impact on the ease of identifying and accessing local support and expertise.

To facilitate this change in educational emphasis there has to be preparation for CPD activity that addresses essential core skills (Goshorn and Fowler Byers, 1997). These activities need to develop critical thinking skills, which enable therapists to identify their learning goals and fully use learning opportunities. The outcomes of these learning opportunities should allow therapists and other interested parties to evaluate the effectiveness of the CPD activities and so facilitate planning of subsequent stages of professional development. The CPD provision has to encompass research values through the use and development of evidence-based practice so that health professionals become critical consumers of all available evidence. To be most effective, the CPD provision needs to be based on sound educational principles that encourage independent learning.

What is needed

In essence, clinical governance and CPD need to be recognized and valued. There is a need for thorough and on-going evaluation of CPD delivery and experience to ensure commitment and quality. It has to be founded on sound educational principles. All stakeholders should have a shared understanding of the factors affecting these activities. Activities need to have the support of all stakeholders in the activities. The effect of specific new initiatives, such as the move to primary care trusts, will also have to be monitored as the reallocation of health professionals into smaller community-based units will have an impact on the ease of identifying and accessing local support and expertise.

There is a need for a CPD package that allows health professionals to support and maintain meaningful lifelong learning. This will require a commitment to a flexible framework that incorporates rigorous validation to ensure that the process is valued by the health professionals, their colleagues and their employers. This must encompass learning for all stages of the career pathway to meet individual and workplace needs.

Maggie McArthur
March 2004

References

Goshorn J, Fowler Byers J (1997) CORE characteristics for survival in patient care redesign. *American Association of Critical Care Nurses* **8**(2): 236–45
Timmreck TC (2001) Managing motivation and developing job satisfaction in the healthcare work environment. *Health Care Manage* **20**(1): 42–58

1

Lifelong learning in healthcare — who pays and who benefits?

Neil Gopee

As the rhetoric of recent decades concerning lifelong learning is gradually translated into practice, we may be seeing the evolution of a learning society in Britain. This long debated concept is now coming to fruition in attempts to identify mechanisms and strategies that promote its implementation. For healthcare professionals this becomes even more important because we are dealing directly with individuals' physical and psychosocial health. While both formal and non-formal learning costs money, non-learning is more costly in terms of skill deficit to the individual and to society. So what is lifelong learning, and who should meet the costs of healthcare staff engaging in lifelong learning?

Perspectives on lifelong learning

The term 'lifelong learning' is now used to encompass the whole range of post-initial education and learning, and therefore includes strategies such as adult education, recurrent education, continuing education, continuing learning, human resource development, continuing vocational education and others.

The concept spans learning that occurs through:
- Formal education — primary to university education
- Non-formal education — organized educational activities outside the formal system
- Informal education — learning that occurs through one's day-to-day life experiences.

More than two decades ago, when the concept was being avidly propounded, Dave (1976) defined lifelong learning as:

> '...a process of accomplishing personal, social and professional development throughout the lifespan of individuals in order to enhance the quality of life of both individuals and their collectives.'

Knapper and Cropley (2000) indicate that lifelong education is:

> '...a set of organizational, financial and didactic principles established with the aim of fostering lifelong learning.'

Gelpi (1985) argues that the concept of lifelong education is temporary, as all active concepts undergo a continuous process of enrichment in terms of interpretation, conception, definition and practice. It is therefore at once a concept, a policy, a practice, a process, a goal and an ideal, and it applies to the whole lifespan of man.

Lifelong learning therefore constitutes a more holistic term, encompassing a broad range of programmes as it is 'one continuous learning system' (Knapper and Cropley, 2000) that includes formal, non-formal and informal learning, as mentioned above, so as to attain the fullest possible development, growth and social progress (Dave, 1976).

Additionally, healthcare professionals work in teams, which provide inherent mechanisms for learning from each other. A positive attitude towards this constitutes one of the characteristics of a learning organization — a popular notion in many large organizations. For patient or client care settings, the English National Board for Nurses, Midwives and Health Visitors (ENB; 1994) identified the key features of a learning organization that contributes to lifelong learning, for example:

- Key stakeholders and practitioners at all levels of the organization are involved in its development
- Staff development and performance review is in place for all practitioners
- Clinical supervision is accessible for practitioners
- Recognition is provided that learning takes place in the workplace
- Commitment is given to encourage reflective practice.

While many of the professions allied to medicine are graduate professions, only a certain proportion of nursing pre-registration courses award a first degree along with the registered nurse qualification. However, one common factor within all such programmes is 'learning to learn' skills, which arm the individual with the expertise for lifelong learning.

A new beginning

The requirement for providing evidence of professional updating for continued professional registration, as implemented by the United Kingdom Central Council for Nurses, Midwives and Health Visitors (UKCC) through post-registration education and practice (PREP), may still be viewed as cumbersome by some health professionals. Besides, Illich and Verne (1976) warned that lifelong learning may constitute 'being imprisoned in the global classroom'. Duke (1976) also expressed some reservation, stating that lifelong education may engender 'a feeling of permanent inadequacy'.

Nevertheless, perceptions change over time and we are increasingly seeing positive attitudes towards lifelong learning. With nurse education now based in higher education and the majority of post-registration modules offered being at diploma level and above, this is a good time for embarking on learning programmes that enable staff to study for diplomas and degrees, including higher degrees.

However, the increasing specialization of most areas of nursing and the continuing evolution of research utilization and evidence-based clinical practice makes continued learning an inherent component of professional employment.

The duration of lifelong learning programmes ranges from postgraduate higher education courses at one end, to informal learning at the other. All are legitimate lifelong learning activities, but Wain (1993) distinguishes between minimalist and maximalist approaches. The minimalist approach equates lifelong education with in-service training, recurrent education and the whole domain of adult education in general. The maximalist approach, on the other hand, sees lifelong education as a fundamental transformation of society, so that the whole of society becomes a learning resource for each individual, and is aware of its educational responsibility.

The year 1996 was designated 'European year of lifelong learning'. To mark this, the ENB organized a symposium that was attended by 40 participants from 12 European countries. The ENB (1998) published a report of the symposium, which documents structures and strategies that are essential to enable healthcare staff to become lifelong learners. This includes involvement of the World Health Organization and International Council for Nurses, and the redirecting of European Union research funding to non-medical healthcare research.

However, it is clear that sources of funding for lifelong learning for healthcare staff are as yet not fully addressed. Titmus (1999) and Tight (1997) recognize that for lifelong learning to be fully functional, individuals must take responsibility for their own learning. In a study exploring the feasibility of implementing lifelong learning, Titmus (1999) found that among the more highly resistant obstacles was the absence of:

> *'...the political will and the sense of urgency that will apparently be required.'*

Inherent to this 'political will' and 'urgency' is the question of who should meet the costs of education for lifelong learning and for meeting PREP requirements.

The UKCC (1994, 2001) recognizes that the implementation of lifelong learning is essential, as PREP requirements may not be sufficient for RNs to maintain up-to-date, appropriate knowledge and competence (eg. Hewlett and Eichelberger, 1996; Gopee, 2001). There is a distinct lack of clarity regarding funding for continuing professional development (CPD) and lifelong learning (Lipley, 2002). According to Coombes (2002), even for developing expanded roles, nurses increasingly have to absorb the costs themselves, without even the guarantee of receiving extra money for taking on the increased responsibility. Coombes reports that despite the rhetoric and expectation for registered nurses to continue developing their roles and engaging in lifelong learning, 'tellingly, no extra government money is attached to the exercise'.

Based on a study of 'investment in post-qualifying education', Calpin-Davies (1999) reports that nursing remains underfunded, and that finding additional funds for non-medical, post-qualifying, professional education should be treated as a priority. Nolan *et al*'s (1995) study of mandatory CPD revealed that CPD does result in improvement in patient care, but staff nurses objected to having to pay for their own CPD as the learning was related to the job, and managers were 'always expecting more for less'.

Dowswell *et al* (1998) used qualitative methods to explore the motives and effects of nurses, midwives and allied professional staff's participation in continuing professional education (CPE). They report that healthcare staff are receiving mixed messages from policy makers and employers about funding for CPE.

A distinction can be made between CPE and CPD, in that the former refers to professional education provided for registered nurses and registered midwives in universities, while the latter encompasses a wide range of professional learning provision and activities (Gopee, 2002). Dowswell *et al* (1998) concluded that if CPE depends on the individual healthcare staff's ability and willingness to pay for post-registration degree-level studies, it is unlikely to be an efficient or equitable means of ensuring lifelong learning for healthcare professions.

The Royal College of Nursing (2002) makes a similar point regarding CPD by indicating that 'funding streams are not clear either for employers obtaining government funding or for individual nurses accessing CPD funds', and those that are available are 'totally uncoordinated'. Thus underfunding of CPD and lifelong learning remains an issue, despite Handy's (1984) recommendation that employers should treat their employees as assets, and invest in them.

Funding for the education of healthcare staff is now the responsibility of the Workforce Development Confederations (Department of Health, 2001a). Workforce Development Confederations and universities are briefed to work in partnership rather than merely as purchasers and providers of CPD courses, respectively. The main reason for establishing this approach is the belief that such work requires collective and collaborative planning, which the previous system did not address.

However, Parish (2002) reports that a single budget for CPD for all groups in the NHS seems to be in the pipeline. It is also anticipated that the *Agenda for Change* venture (Department of Health, 2002), linking pay to competencies, and the arrival of the NHS University in October 2003 (Department of Health, 2001b) will play some role towards rectifying this anomaly.

Conclusions

It appears that the attitude that is essential for most nurses and healthcare staff to undertake CPE and lifelong learning is already shifting in the correct direction. This should be a major milestone that establishes a framework for both CPE during one's career, and lifelong education within the whole spectrum encompassing one's working life and post-retirement. This would realize the emphasis on lifelong learning advocated in the Dearing Report (National Committee of Inquiry into Higher Education, 1997).

Such experience of continuing self-actualization and fulfilment can be seen as both the right and the desire of all individuals, healthcare staff and their clientele.

References

Calpin-Davies P (1999) Investing in the future. *Nurs Manage* **5**(9): 17–23

Coombes R (2002) The advanced practice payment scandal. *Nurs Times* **98**(49): 10–11

Dave RH (1976) *Foundations of Lifelong Education*. Pergamon Press, Oxford

Department of Health (2001a) *Workforce Development Confederations Guidance — Functions of a Mature Confederation*. DoH, London

Department of Health (2001b) *Working Together, Learning Together*. DoH, London

Department of Health (2002) *Agenda for Change — Modernising the NHS Pay System*. DoH, London

Dowswell T, Hewison J, Hinds M (1998) Motivational forces affecting participation in post-registration degree courses and effects on home and work life: a qualitative study. *J Adv Nurs* **28**(6): 1326–33

Duke C (1976) *Lifelong Education: an Australian Perspective*. Australian National University, Canberra

English National Board (1994) *Creating Lifelong Learners*. END, London

English National Board (1998) *Lifelong Learning in Europe: Developing a Strategic Approach*. ENB, London

Gelpi E (1985) *Lifelong Education and International Relations*. Croom Helm Ltd, Kent

Gopee N (2001) Nurses' perceptions of PREP. *Prof Nurs* **16**(6): 1139

Gopee N (2002) Impact of continuing professional education — an analysis of a management course. *Nurs Manage* **8**(9): 21–5

Handy C (1984) *The Future of Work: a Guide to a Changing Society*. Blackwell Science, Oxford

Hewlett PO, Eichelberger LW (1996) The case against mandatory continuing education. *J Contin Educ Nurs* **27**(4): 176–81

Illich I, Verne E (1976) *Imprisoned in a Global Classroom*. Writers and Readers Publishing Company, London

Knapper CK, Cropley AJ (2000) *Lifelong Learning in Higher Education*. 3rd edn. Kogan Page, London

Lipley N (2002) Goodbye to PREP. *Nurs Stand* **16**(30): 13

National Committee of Inquiry into Higher Education (1997) *Higher Education in the Learning Society*. NCIHE, London

Nolan M, Owens RG, Nolan J (1995) Continuing professional education: identifying the characteristics of an effective system. *J Adv Nurs* **21**: 551–60

Parish C (2002) Single budget for all staff groups in CPD shake-up. *Nurs Stand* **16**(44): 4

Royal College of Nursing (2002) *Quality Education for Quality Care: a Position Statement for Nursing Education*. RCN, London

Tight M (1997) Career as a concept and experience. *Adults Learn* **9**(2): 22–4

Titmus C (1999) Concepts and practices of education and adult education: obstacles to lifelong education and lifelong learning. *Int J Lifelong Educ* **18**(3): 343–54

United Kingdom Central Council for Nursing, Midwifery and Health Visiting (1994) *The Future of Professional Practice: the Council's Standards for Education and Practice Following Registration*. UKCC, London

United Kingdom Central Council for Nursing, Midwifery and Health Visiting (2001) *Supporting Nurses, Midwives and Health Visitors Through Lifelong Learning*. UKCC, London

Wain K (1993) Lifelong education and adult education — the state of the theory. *Int J Lifelong Educ* **12**(2): 85–99

Key points

❉ Lifelong learning is a holistic term that encompasses continuing professional education (CPE) and learning undertaken by formal, non-formal and informal means so as to attain the fullest possible development, growth and social progress.

❉ It appears that the attitude that is essential for most nurses and healthcare staff to undertake CPE and lifelong learning is already shifting in the correct direction. This should be a major milestone that establishes a framework for both CPE during one's career, and lifelong education within the whole spectrum encompassing one's working life and post-retirement.

❉ Lifelong education costs money, but its absence is even more costly in terms of skill requirement and self-fulfilment.

❉ It is clear that sources of funding for lifelong learning for healthcare staff are as yet not fully addressed.

2

The place of portfolios within continuing professional development

Sandra Stewart

This chapter looks at a possible model of continuing professional development (CPD), as suggested at a conference on professional development held at the University of East Anglia in September 1997. It puts CPD into the framework of legislative changes affecting the professions supplementary to medicine, and then explores how CPD might be taken forward by healthcare professionals as a process-based activity. This ensures that therapists are not only taking responsibility for identifying their own learning needs, but also provides evidence that CPD is taking place. Subsequent chapters discuss particular 'tools' for CPD, to which this chapter alludes.

Introduction

Health professionals face a more challenging working environment than ever before, as they now work in a complex area where both policy and practice have changed considerably over the past few decades. New advances in knowledge and technology impact on the workforce alongside pressures to meet performance targets in terms of both quality and quantity. The public expect high standards of quality in their treatment and integrity in those health professionals delivering it (Health Professions Council, 2002). Such widespread changes in healthcare delivery have led to the reform of the regulatory regimens that have governed health professionals for the past three decades.

Health Professions Council

The Health Professions Order 2001 is the statutory instrument arising out of the Health Act 1999 that underpins the new Health Professions Council (HPC), which has replaced the Council for Professions Supplementary to Medicine (CPSM). This new council has been designed to provide a modern regulatory framework for the 12 health professions previously regulated by the CPSM. Council membership consists of 12 registrant members (professionals on the register) who are elected by the professions, and 11 lay members appointed by the privy council.

The aim of this new regulator is to safeguard the health and well-being of anyone using or needing the services of these professionals by reforming the ways of working and by reforming structure and functions (Department of Health, 2001). It is within the second remit that the HPC will be specifically addressing issues around fitness to practice.

The HPC is charged with the responsibility for specifying and monitoring the standards of professional education and the performance and conduct of its members, for providing stronger protection of professional roles and for linking registration with evidence of continuing professional development (CPD).

The duties of the HPC include:

- Establishing and maintaining a register
- Specifying and monitoring standards of education and training at all stages
- Specifying and monitoring standards of conduct, performance and ethics
- Investigating allegations against professionals and taking action to ensure the protection of the public
- Carrying out other duties that support these functions.

Four statutory cross-professional committees now undertake the bulk of these duties:

- The Investigating Committee (a practice committee), which deals with initial complaints
- The Conduct and Competence Committee (a practice committee), whose remit is to consider standards of conduct and appropriate disciplinary procedures for misconduct
- The Health Committee (a practice committee), which deals with cases where a registrant is thought to be unfit to practise because of physical or mental ill health
- The Education and Training Committee, which is responsible for advising and acting on behalf of the HPC in all aspects of education, qualifications, registration criteria and CPD. As part of its functions it is expected to consult with professional bodies and other relevant interests to issue guidelines for CPD programmes and ensure they meet HPC criteria.

On advice from the Education and Training Committee, the HPC will determine strategy and set out policy and guidelines for the type of CPD programmes that should be followed, and also on the need for internship and mentoring programmes.

CPD and health professionals

Implicit in the notion of public protection is the concept that registered health professionals are indeed competent to practise. One of the weaknesses of the Professions Supplementary to Medicine (PSM) Act (1960) was that registration could be for life without the need for practitioners ever to demonstrate that they were:

- Keeping up-to-date
- Competent
- Medically fit to practise.

Within the codes of conduct of each professional group are statements relating to maintaining competence to practise (eg. Chartered Society of Physiotherapy (CSP), 1996; College of Occupational Therapists (COT), 1995), but these are quite separate from registration procedures.

The HPC has now stipulated that evidence of CPD will be a requirement to maintain state registration, and registrants who have not practiced for a period of time will be required to undertake education and training to retain or regain registration.

The detail and structure of such programmes is still being established following discussions held between the Education and Training Committee, the relevant professional bodies and other relevant stakeholders.

From consultations to date, the strongest emerging theme has been the need for mandatory, evidence-based CPD schemes, with the majority of respondents in favour of practitioners maintaining a portfolio or log of professional development linked to the periodic renewal of registration (Department of Health, 2001).

CPD: process or product?

For the full potential of CPD to be realized, health professionals required to produce evidence of continuing development will need to have a sense of ownership of their own CPD. Pessimistically, it seems possible that CPD might almost become a standardized product — a list of competencies and behaviours, perhaps informed by a series of short courses (either in-house or provided by an educational establishment), which therapists 'tick off' on an inventory as part of their portfolio.

The purpose of this more traditional model is knowledge acquisition with the assumption that change will arise from a standardized knowledge base. The process is didactic — instructors are 'experts' and the practitioner is a passive, subordinate consumer (Osterman and Kottkamp, 1993). Such a reductionist approach might ensure that all therapists attain a particular level of clinical competence, but even that may be disputed (Craik, 1997); it does not really allow individuals to respond creatively and well to the changing demands of health care.

Health care is a rapidly changing environment, thus health practitioners must be able to stay abreast of both the changing work setting and new ideas within their own profession, as well as understand how such ideas impinge on their own practice. Buzz-words of the 1990s have included terms such as 'reflective practice' and 'life-long learning'. CPD is viewed as life-long learning, an individual process rather than a product, and is much more likely to enable practitioners to meet the challenges of their working environment.

When CPD is regarded as an active exploration of individual learning needs, using reflective practice and other strategies to provide deeper insights into current professional performance, it becomes much more creative and empowering, enabling practitioners to challenge and change outmoded methods of working and ensuring their own clinical effectiveness. Such a model assumes that change arises out of self-awareness, with the practitioner much more an action researcher than a passive consumer of knowledge.

Reflective practice in a process model of CPD

Reflective practice has variously been defined as the:

> *'Practitioner's ability to access, make sense of and learn through work experience to achieve more desirable, effective and satisfying work' (Johns, 1995),*

or

> *'The process of internally examining and exploring an issue of concern, triggered by an experience that creates and clarifies meaning in terms of self, and that results in a changed conceptual perspective' (Boyd and Fales, 1983).*

A more detailed discussion of reflection and how to undertake it is given in *Chapter 5*, but at this point it is worth noting that reflection is fundamental in underpinning a process model of CPD:

- It provides an opportunity to critically evaluate current practice and identify what is being learnt and what needs to change
- It enables experiences in the workplace to become experiential learning and not simply to remain experiences (Kolb, 1984)
- It facilitates the identification of individual learning needs, which can then be actioned appropriately.

Reflective practice is best supported by a range of other tools and strategies (see other chapters). In discussing either CPD or reflective practice, authors have identified a number of other options that may also prove useful (Alsop, 2000; Hull and Redfern, 1996).

Providing the evidence: the place for portfolios

It is suggested that when these tools and strategies are used regularly, and particularly when the process is recorded as in writing up a critical incident, an individual builds up a body of evidence that clearly demonstrates professional development. A health professional using a process model of CPD should be relatively well placed to provide sufficient material for the requirements of state registration annually, provided it is presented in a clear and concise manner, such as within a portfolio.

In addressing the issue of CPD, most professional bodies (eg. the CSP and the COT) have published documentation to assist therapists in structuring and formally recording their own CPD. The use of portfolios underpins the presentation of such evidence.

Portfolios and the purpose behind them

Brown (1995) defines a portfolio as:

> '...a private collection of evidence that demonstrates the continuing acquisition of skills, knowledge, attitudes, understanding and achievements. It is both retrospective and prospective, as well as reflecting the current stage of development and activity of the individual.'

Others have suggested that keeping a portfolio should be more than merely a recording device — it is a way of developing skills of critical reflective practice, and considering and evaluating how experiences in both professional and personal life contribute to improvements in patient care (English National Board, 1991). Such a concept fits well with a process model of CPD.

The emphasis on the word 'private' indicates that portfolios are for personal use only, and should therefore be used as a database to collect and collate evidence of both professional and personal development. It is a document over which the individual has total control, deciding what should be included and how that information should be formatted. However, the overriding consideration should be that the contents sum up professional life to date (Lillyman and Evans, 1996).

Portfolios, profiles or diaries?

Brown (1995) defines 'profiles' as:

> *'...a collection of evidence that is selected from the personal portfolio for a particular purpose and for the attention of a particular audience.'*

The CSP discusses professional development documentation for physiotherapists in terms of 'diaries', while the COT uses the term professional development 'portfolios', and both professional bodies have formal documents using those titles. Elsewhere, health practitioners use the various terms interchangeably, but all organizations are referring to a process and a product that seeks to provide evidence of CPD using relatively similar formats.

Defining profiles. A profile, using Brown's definition, may well be the appropriate document to produce for maintaining state registration. It is anticipated that the items within such a profile would change from year to year, and may well be a selection from a much wider body of available evidence contained within a personal portfolio; nevertheless, it should still meet the criteria of being clear, concise and coherent.

In principle, a profile could be used for a variety of purposes, both academic and professional. For an individual it is a recognized means of providing evidence that demonstrates competence for certification of work-based learning, for example: supporting an 'accreditation of prior learning' application for entry to a degree programme; or it may be used to demonstrate knowledge for a job application or promotion.

Defining portfolios. Portfolio development is regarded as an appropriate way to provide evidence of experiential learning by most health professions. Much has been written about experiential learning (Kolb, 1984; Weil and McGill, 1990; Boud *et al*, 1993; Eraut and Cole, 1993), and all suggest that experience is much more than mere observation. Present experience is linked with previous knowledge and experience and combined uniquely in a given individual. The same experience will not be given the same meaning by different people, nor will they achieve similar learning outcomes.

Compiling a portfolio serves the useful function of enabling individuals to reflect on how and what is learnt and to demonstrate an understanding and appreciation of the significance of that learning. An ongoing process of reflection enhances self-awareness and builds confidence in the value of life and experience to date.

Thorpe (1993) suggests that writing is a way of capturing thoughts and feelings and of structuring and using reflection strategically for intentional learning. Recording both the reasoning process and the learning outcomes is likely to provide a more systematic way of reviewing experiences, of clarifying what has been learnt and of making a permanent record of the process itself for future reference. The actual development of a portfolio requires some of these processes to occur, but it is likely that individuals who use reflective practice techniques will find that much of their learning is already being systematically recorded (*Chapter 5* considers this issue in more depth).

The process of creating a portfolio

In its *Professional Development Diary*, the CSP (1992) has stated that:

> *'Portfolio preparation is an exercise in self-evaluation, organization and integration, requiring you to relate past learning and to demonstrate an ability to present documentation in a clear and concise manner.'*

Other key features are that it should be selective while remaining coherent, and that each section should stand alone but be cross-referenced to other sections of the portfolio.

There is no single correct format for a portfolio, but it is likely that it will commence with a résumé or *curriculum vitae* detailing your educational and vocational history to date, as well as indicating your leisure pursuits and the range of skills you bring to your present job. This aspect of the portfolio is likely to be descriptive — a scene-setting exercise detailing events and achievements rather than identifying what has been learnt from them.

Following on from that descriptive presentation, it is likely that you will then want to include a statement that gives a clear idea of where you are now, in terms of:

- Your current experience, skills and knowledge base
- Your current objectives, both personally and professionally — the experience, skills and knowledge you still want to acquire
- Some idea of your long-term goals, ie. a one-year and a five-year development plan.

As mentioned earlier, there are a number of 'tools' that should enable you to compile documents for use in your portfolio. When used selectively, these strategies can help you to:

- Identify appropriate learning outcomes
- Reflect on experiences across a wide range of settings
- Demonstrate your personal growth and professional development.

Within a process model of CPD these tools should become so familiar to you for identifying learning needs that you would use them routinely to ensure your CPD.

The aim of a portfolio is to provide a collection of evidence that demonstrates the continued acquisition of knowledge, skills and achievements. It should be reflective and critical, demonstrating how and what has been learnt and how it can be applied in different situations. However, it is also personal to an individual, and therefore will not necessarily look the same or contain similar information to the portfolios of other professionals.

References

Alsop A (2000) *Continuing Professional Development*. Blackwell Science, Oxford

Boud D, Cohen R, Walker D, eds (1993) *Using Experience for Learning.* Society for Research in Higher Education/Open University Press, Buckingham

Boyd E, Fales A (1983) Reflecting learning: key to learning from experience. *J Human Psychol* **23**: 99–117

Brown R (1995) *Portfolio Development and Profiling for Nurses.* 2nd edn. Quay Books, Dinton

Chartered Society of Physiotherapy (1992) *Professional Development Diary — Section Two (iv).* CSP, London

Chartered Society of Physiotherapy (1996) *Rules of Professional Conduct.* CSP, London

College of Occupational Therapists (1995) *Code of Ethics and Professional Conduct for Occupational Therapists.* COT, London

Craik C (1997) Review of the Professions Supplementary to Medicine Act 1960. *Br J Occup Ther* **60**(7): 309–14

Department of Health (2001) *Establishing the New Health Professions Council.* DoH, London

English Nursing Board (1991) *Professional Portfolio.* ENB Publications, London

Eraut M, Cole G (1993) Assessment of competence in higher level occupations. *Competence Assess* **21**: 10–14

Health Professions Council (2002) *The Future: a Mini Prospectus.* HPC, London

Hull C, Redfern L (1996) *Profiles and Portfolios.* Macmillan, London

Johns C (1995) The value of reflective practice for nursing. *J Clin Nursing* **4**: 23–40

Kolb D (1984) *Experiential Learning: Experience as a Source of Learning and Development.* Prentice-Hall, New Jersey

Lillyman S, Evans B (1996) *Designing a Personal Portfolio/Profile: A Workbook for Healthcare Professionals.* Quay Books, Dinton

Osterman K, Kottkamp R (1993) *Reflective Practice for Educators — Improving Schooling Through Professional Development.* Sage, London

Thorpe M (1993) Experiential learning at a distance. In: Boud D, Cohen R, Walker D, eds. *Using Experience for Learning.* Society of Research into Higher Education/Open University Press, Buckingham

Weil S, McGill I (1990) (eds) *Making Sense of Experiential Learning.* Society of Research into Higher Education/Open University Press, Buckingham

Key points

✣ Healthcare professionals now practise in a constantly changing environment, as new advances in knowledge and technology impact on the workforce alongside pressures to meet performance targets in terms of both quality and quantity.

✣ Such widespread changes in healthcare delivery have led to the reform of the regulatory regimens that have governed health professionals for the past three decades.

✣ The Health Professions Council (HPC) is charged with the responsibility for specifying and monitoring the standards of professional education and the performance and conduct of its members, for providing stronger protection of professional roles and for linking registration with evidence of continuing professional development (CPD).

✣ The HPC has now stipulated that evidence of CPD will be a requirement to maintain state registration, and registrants who have not practised for a period of time will be required to undertake education and training to retain or regain registration.

✣ CPD is viewed as life-long learning, an individual process rather than a product, and is much more likely to enable practitioners to meet the challenges of their working environment.

✣ In addressing the issue of CPD, most professional bodies have published documentation to assist therapists in structuring and formally recording their own CPD. The use of portfolios underpins the presentation of such evidence.

3

Can clinical reasoning be an effective tool in continuing professional development?

Richard Stephenson

This chapter continues looking at possible models of continuing professional development (CPD). The potential for clinical reasoning as a tool in exploring and analysing professional development is discussed, with particular reference to Higgs' concept of cognitive mapping. It is suggested that through the construction and analysis of 'problem' maps, deficits and strengths in the knowledge and skills used to solve the problem can be identified. Collaborative analysis with a mentor or peer group could enhance individuals' understanding of their reasoning ability. This enables the therapist to determine areas of practice where development is required and to implement a plan for CPD. Where this information is used as part of appraisal, it serves as a focus for negotiated and supported activity leading to CPD.

Introduction

A conference on continuing professional development (CPD) held at the University of East Anglia explored the role of clinical reasoning in professional practice and considered the opportunity to use the reasoning process as an analytical tool to determine professional needs. This chapter does not address the theoretical basis of clinical reasoning, but outlines the areas discussed at that workshop, and proposes a model of CPD that would be sensitive to all professionals, leading to increased effectiveness in whatever domain that individual practices.

Reasoning in clinical practice

Devlin (1991) uses an analogy to explore the logic of information. This is modified to offer an insight into clinical reasoning:

> *Consider travelling back in time to encounter an ironsmith. The ironsmith is a master of his profession, renowned among peers and public alike for the beauty of his work. He has trained many apprentice ironsmiths who have gone on to develop similar mastery. The ironsmith knows nothing of the molecular structure of iron, nor does he conceive of such a theory, but he knows a good piece of iron! He also knows how to heat and hit iron into shape, and yet he knows nothing of what he does to the iron or why the intervention is successful. Similarly, his apprentices watch and learn the technique, developing mastery of their craft, but cannot express their skill in any verbal or written form.*

The history of the health professions is dominated by such practice. Clinical problems have been solved by a whole array of strategies, often without a clear understanding of why or how those strategies have been successful. The practitioner learns to solve similar problems in similar ways; intervention is determined by knowledge of past results and modified to meet new situations by comparison of present feedback with that of the past. This knowledge becomes embodied in the intuitive skill of the craftsman, producing highly skilled clinicians, although they are like the ironsmith above.

Without the ability to make explicit clinicians' knowledge, their reasoning cannot be questioned; if it cannot be questioned it cannot be understood. It produces a 'watch and learn' approach to therapy, restricting professional development (of the individual and the profession) to an inductive practice. It fails to enable a deductive approach, where new treatment can be generated based on the prevailing theoretical understanding.

What is clinical reasoning?

Clinical reasoning is defined as:

> *'The thinking and decision-making processes that are integral to clinical practice' (Higgs and Jones, 1995a).*

The simplicity of the definition, however, belies that it is the essential feature of professional practice, which moves the practitioner from technician (at the instruction of a decision maker) to autonomous professional. The underpinning reasoning of all clinical intervention is the fundamental ground upon which professional clinical efficacy is built. Where reasoning is absent, treatment is placed in the realm of guesswork and becomes the domain of habit (at best) or whim and fancy (at worst). The clearer the process and content of clinical reasoning during any intervention, the more able professionals will be to make explicit their decision-making process. Numerous models of clinical reasoning exist, although these will not be covered here (see Wolf, 1985; Mattingly, 1991a,b; Mattingly and Fleming, 1994; Higgs and Jones, 1995a).

Cognitive mapping

Higgs (1992a,b, 1993) has developed the concept of cognitive mapping. This enables the practitioner to take a clinical episode and identify the theoretical and practical knowledge, skills and evidence that should be considered (and used) when attempting to implement an effective therapeutic strategy. It is perhaps easiest to follow this type of reasoning through a series of examples.

Figure 3.1 takes us back to elementary mathematics and identifies a problem to be solved. How far is the ship from the base of the lighthouse? To successfully address this problem, the 'clinician' uses several schema of knowledge, all of which contribute to an understanding of Pythagoras' theorem.

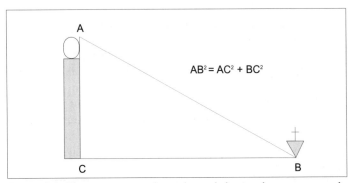

Figure 3.1. If we recognize the right-angled triangle, we can apply Pythagoras' theorem to determine the distance of any 'side', providing we know the length of the other two 'sides'.

Figure 3.2 maps some of the component schema of this theorem that have to be understood to comprehend the whole; concepts of triangles, right angles, square roots, basic numeracy, hypotenuse, etc. As can be seen, some of these schema are related in such a way as to form sub-concepts of larger concepts; the component schema have to be understood in order to construct the larger schema. For example, to understand a right angle requires an understanding of angles, degrees and general principles of geometry. In solving the problem, 'clinicians' have to be certain that the evidence they use to construct each schema is reliable and valid. They also have to recognize that the schema have to be related and assimilated in order to solve the problem; unless all the concepts are used to inform each other, the solution will not be found.

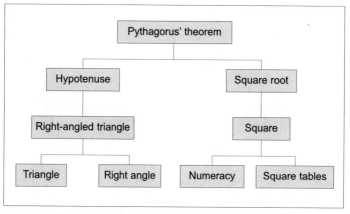

Figure 3.2. The conceptual schema used to understand Pythagoras' theorem can be mapped. Note that each schema can be broken down further into basic subunits, but it will require all the schema to understand the main concept. Where one schema is absent, poorly understood or inappropriately applied, the whole concept will be inadequately understood.

Figure 3.3 considers some of the basic schema that might be considered by a therapist when addressing a clinical problem. The components identified are by no means exhaustive, and for different problems will require different areas of knowledge. Each schema could be further 'mapped' to explore all the components within it; thus, a physiotherapist's professional skills may include communication, teaching, management, patient handling, motivation and a whole array of therapeutic activities that will be based on further schema. It is essential, however, that the therapist recognizes the vast array of skills and areas of knowledge that are used in considering a basic, 'everyday' problem.

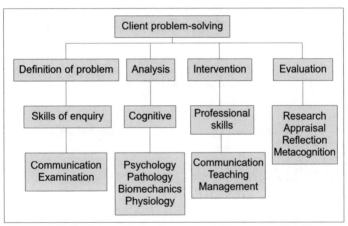

Figure 3.3. Only the very basic of conceptual schema are offered here to illustrate a few areas of professional knowledge used in clinical problem-solving and decision-making. A conceptual domain such as anatomy (not identified here) would need further mapping: sub-units could be traced down a hierarchy of concepts such as joint, synovial, articular, cartilage, hyaline cartilage, collagen, chondroblasts, cellular form and function. For each 'level' cross-reference into other domains would occur, such as physiology, biomechanics and pathology.

Figure 3.4 takes a type of map (again kept as simple as possible) a stage further and looks at one 'simple' clinical problem. You may wish to construct your own map for the same problem! Further clinical examples are provided by Higgs (1992a).

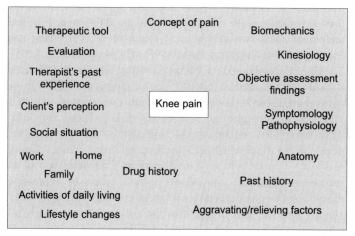

Figure 3.4. A basic map of some key concepts relating to the understanding of 'knee pain'. Again, each conceptual schema would be refined into smaller subunits, all of which require understanding if the central concept is to be fully understood.

Cognitive mapping can be used to assist therapists in addressing their knowledge and skill base in relation to practice. By exploring clinical problems and identifying the components that are involved in addressing the problem, therapists begin to make explicit what it is they know and what it is they use when carrying out 'therapy'.

This reflection on practice enables therapists to question the validity of their knowledge base. It allows therapists to see where schema should be assimilated and how aspects of theory and practice intermesh into cohesive and consistent practice. It enables therapists to question what has hitherto been nebulously defined as intuition or tacit-embodied knowledge, by identifying exactly where each aspect of intervention originates and what evidence supports their action (including the validity of that support). To do this, however, therapists require skills of metacognition: the ability to analyse and understand their own thinking and cognitive skills (Fleming and Mattingly, 1994; Higgs and Jones, 1995b; Higgs and Titchen, 1995).

Once the embodied (or tacit) knowledge used by the clinician is explored and made explicit it can be questioned: if it can be questioned, it can be understood. From this understanding comes diagnosis of strengths and deficiencies in knowledge and skills. This awareness becomes the foundation for professional development (individual and profession wide). Thus, clinical reasoning (particularly cognitive mapping) becomes a tool to explore professional 'know-how': it is a means of addressing everything that clinicians take with them into the clinical problem-solving episode; and it identifies the solid, reasoned, decision-making process and the potential deficiencies in evidence and ability in any aspect of their role.

Whither CPD?

Problems with mapping

A potential problem with mapping and other tools of clinical reasoning is the implicit Fabian notion that suggests the activity will lead to enlightenment and change. There is, however, a real danger that novices to clinical reasoning will carry out the activity but fail to establish whether the 'chunks' of content identified in their map are sound or weak. They may fail to recognize that they need specific skills, or may be ignorant of the knowledge required. More commonly, they may lack the skills of metacognition required to fully understand how they constructed the map and what to do with it. Thus, the activity does not lead to enlightenment but a perpetuation of the status quo; all the evidence used is sound, the skills are clearly identified and practised with great efficiency, but as there is no recognition of other potential influences, there is no sense that any change must occur. For these reasons, a mentor or peer-review process applied to clinical reasoning may be beneficial.

Role of a mentor

Consider a model wherein clinical reasoning becomes a tool of analysis used to identify what clinicians require to operate effectively at their level of problem-solving. The tool is primarily employed by the individual, but the reasoning made explicit to others, possibly peers, senior professionals or a mentor (an expert guide). This exploration of the reasoning process and findings identifies what therapists hold as strengths and weaknesses based upon their development to date, and offers areas of future development that could address their specific needs.

At this point we should substitute clinical reasoning for professional reasoning. Thus, it would be highly appropriate for a professional to have needs that would be based in management skills, service development, educational theory or research, and not merely in clinical intervention. This form of reasoning would be equally applicable to all areas.

The tool could become formalized as part of the appraisal process (individual performance review, or whatever terminology is used). Individuals use the reasoning process on a series of practice-specific problems (with mentor support) to establish their specific needs (emerging themes), which, if satisfied, would better enable them to operate more efficiently in their professional field. As such it becomes a means of formulating the required process of professional development and identifying clear objectives or goals associated with enhanced practice. It would identify the end-point and the process that would achieve this.

End-points may be achievable in differing time scales and would be both short- and long-term development goals. A learning (or development) contract could then be constructed that addressed these needs and aims, and identified the process through which development would be pursued. The activities of development may require monitoring and evaluation via a great many media, such as a reflective (professional) diary or portfolio (Alsop, 1997).

Benefits of clinical reasoning in appraisal

There are two major benefits of such a system. First, professionals generate their own criteria for development. Professional development becomes a highly personal activity, while the review process recognizes ('authorizes') that the logic and plan used is professionally appropriate and relevant. Peer review need not mean uni-professional; there may be benefits should other professionals consider the reasoning process. A different perspective on the reasoning employed, or the potential application and content of the identified (or non-identified) chunks, might generate new professional interpretations and suggest novel directions for development. It would also place the plan for development into a realistic context of what is available and could be supported in the particular environment.

Second, by not having a system of prescribed development imposed upon the individual (in the form of professional standards or a predetermined route), it might be that the therapist generates a need for new areas of development that were not previously part of the reasoning process. Providing that the logic is sound and can be justified to their peers, such new development could be pursued, leading to change.

The focus is placed on the process of development in achieving self-directed (but professionally monitored) aims; these will often be common across many professionals of similar development, but will also include highly specific, individual direction.

Conclusions

CPD is not an option — the code of conduct for each professional group contains some statement relating to maintaining competence to practice (eg. rule 1 of the Chartered Society of Physiotherapy code of conduct (Chartered Society of Physiotherapy, 1996); rule 5.4 of the College of Occupational Therapists code of conduct (College of Occupational Therapists, 1995).

It is the responsibility of individuals to systematically analyse and identify their development and competence (Coates, 1997); CPD covers the whole gamut of formal and informal learning, and is inextricably linked to the context of practice (Eraut, 1994).

There are, however, many stakeholders with an interest in CPD and, therefore, many potential masters (*Figure 3.5*).

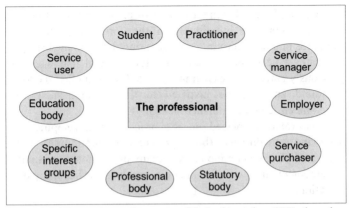

Figure 3.5. The professional is responsible for his or her CPD; the other stakeholders have a vested interest in the CPD that the professional undertakes. The primary requirements of CPD identified by each stakeholder may be different, and potential conflict exists.

It is possible that each stakeholder requires different things from the professional, and would wish to structure CPD accordingly. Consider the potential conflict in trying to satisfy the role required of you by clients, employers, students, specific interest groups, your professional body or the Council for Professions Supplementary to Medicine, and the criteria each may apply when determining whether your competence is meeting their expectations. It is, therefore, important that professionals take a key role in determining their destiny; indeed, this is essential to retain autonomy.

Possible bases for CPD

CPD could be product- or process-based; the two are not necessarily incompatible, but they could be. There is a need to facilitate development (process) and measure change (product).

CPD could be seen as a short-term or long-term activity. Development is lifelong, but there is often a desire to see immediate achievement. CPD could be self-determined or it could be imposed, dictating how each individual must develop towards a predetermined set point (a sort of norm-referenced profession). Each potential master has a view on these possible structures.

At worst, CPD will be developed as a product-based system that defines the product via a series of behaviours or standards that each individual adheres to. The profession, therefore, moves towards a standardized, uniform and measurable, predetermined state. This is a closed system that perpetuates the profession as it exists; the standards are defined by what exists now and cannot easily incorporate potential change. In effect, such a system restricts development and 'dwarfs' the profession.

At best, CPD will be process-based, where professionals negotiate their own specific development through a declaration of their needs and a justification of their aims and proposed activities to their peers. It will empower the individual, offering self-direction (within reasonable, professionally determined boundaries), with the potential to move beyond present practice. It will enable creativity and originality in thought and action, taking the individual and the profession into new dimensions. This can be measured, but it requires a time-scale appropriate for change.

Potential for CPD

The potential role for clinical reasoning in the latter model of CPD is vast. It could become the tool through which CPD is investigated and needs are determined. The peer-review process and the need to fully understand reasoning becomes paramount if confidence in the process is to be established. It is, however, a tool that can be used by all professionals, irrespective of their expertise and area of practice. It allows CPD to develop via the mastery of one tool by all professional groups. It offers a forum for multiprofessional discourse and analysis of practice with the potential for cross-fertilization of ideas and knowledge. Most importantly, it gives meaning to CPD and ensures that vital energy is channelled into activities that the professional 'owns', rather than into the collection of specific 'points' required in the next 12 months.

In the absence of an all-encompassing system that uses clinical reasoning as a tool of CPD, the above model remains a highly worthwhile activity for individuals, departments and professional groups. It opens for discussion whole areas of the knowledge base, and allows for that knowledge to be questioned and critically evaluated.

It can be a threat for the individual to make explicit their strengths and weaknesses, and to this end the mentor system should explore the real depth of understanding in the individual. As a group activity, however, the focus placed upon a specific area of common involvement provides a major facilitation to multiprofessional understanding and an arena for shared development.

Acknowledgements

The author would like to thank all those who participated in the workshop at the conference, and Dr Geoffery Kidd for earlier discussions and collaboration on the use of mapping and reasoning in developing professional understanding.

References

Alsop A (1997) Evidence-based practice and continuing professional development. *Br J Occup Ther* **60**: 503–8

Chartered Society of Physiotherapy (1996) *Rules of Professional Conduct.* Chartered Society of Physiotherapy, London

Coates M (1997) Much more than this.... *Health Management* **September**: 10–13

College of Occupational Therapists (1995) *Code of Ethics and Professional Conduct for Occupational Therapists.* College of Occupational Therapists, London

Devlin K (1991) *Logic and Information.* Cambridge University Press, Cambridge

Eraut M (1994) *Developing Professional Knowledge and Competence.* Falmer Press, London

Fleming MH, Mattingly C (1994) Giving language to practice. In: Mattingly C, Fleming MH, eds. *Clinical Reasoning: Forms of Inquiry in a Therapeutic Practice.* FA Davies, Philadelphia: 3–21

Higgs J (1992a) Developing clinical reasoning competencies. *Physiotherapy* **78**: 575–81

Higgs J (1992b) Developing knowledge: a process of construction mapping and review. *NZ J Physiother* **August**: 23–30

Higgs J (1993) A programme for developing clinical reasoning skills in graduate physiotherapists. *Medical Teacher* **15**: 195–205

Higgs J, Jones M, eds (1995a) *Clinical Reasoning in the Health Professions.* Butterworth Heinemann, Oxford

Higgs J, Jones M (1995b) Clinical reasoning. In: Higgs J, Jones M, eds. *Clinical Reasoning in the Health Professions.* Butterworth Heinemann, Oxford: 3–23

Higgs J, Titchen A (1995) Propositional, professional and personal knowledge in clinical reasoning. In: Higgs J, Jones M, eds. *Clinical Reasoning in the Health Professions.* Butterworth Heinemann, Oxford: 129–46

Mattingly C (1991a) What is clinical reasoning? *Am J Occup Ther* **45**: 979–86

Mattingly C (1991b) The narrative of clinical reasoning. *Am J Occup Ther* **45**: 998–1005

Mattingly C, Fleming MH, eds (1994) *Clinical Reasoning: Forms of Inquiry in a Therapeutic Practice.* FA Davies, Philadelphia

Wolf SL, ed (1985) *Clinical Decision-Making in Physical Therapy.* FA Davies, Philadelphia

Key points

⌘ Clinical reasoning is a tool for exploring work-related (real or potential) problems, and is applicable to all professional groups.

⌘ The clearer the process and content of clinical reasoning during any intervention, the more able professionals will be to make explicit their decision-making process.

⌘ The tool can be used as an individual exercise, as a peer exercise or in conjunction with an experienced mentor.

⌘ Because the tool is work based, and conclusions only relate to the individual context, it is a highly meaningful tool for identifying CPD needs.

⌘ Clinical reasoning allows CPD to develop via the mastery of one tool by all professional groups. It offers a forum for multiprofessional discourse and analysis of practice with the potential for cross-fertilization of ideas and knowledge.

⌘ Most importantly, clinical reasoning gives meaning to CPD and ensures that vital energy is channelled into activities that the professional 'owns', rather than into the collection of specific 'points' required in the next 12 months.

4

Using critical incidents to enhance CPD: mentor and student perspectives

Chia Swee Hong, Emma Payne

Reflection is a fundamental component in the process of continuing professional development (CPD). Reflective practice is best supported by a range of tools including critical incident analysis, which is the focus of this chapter. Critical incidents may be used as part of a personal portfolio/profile. They can be used to explore the links between theory and practice, and provide strategies for coping with similar incidents in the future. A case study is presented by an occupational therapy student, putting theory into practice.

Introduction

Reflection is a fundamental component in the process of CPD. Reflective practice has been defined as:

> '...the process of internally examining and exploring an issue of concern, triggered by an experience that creates and clarifies meaning in terms of self, and which results in a changed conceptual perspective' (Boyd and Fales, 1983).

Tools for continuing professional development

It is not enough simply for us to experience a critical incident in order to learn. It is our reflection of the incident that helps learning and development to take place. Gibbs (1988) adds:

> 'This learning must be tested out in new situations. The learner must make the link between theory and action by planning for that action, carrying it out, and then reflecting upon it, relating what happens back to the theory.'

In *Chapter 2* of this book, 'The place of portfolios within continuing professional development' (pp. 14–15), Sandra Stewart maintains that:

> 'When CPD is regarded as an active exploration of individual learning needs, using reflective practice and other strategies to provide deeper insights into current professional performance, it becomes much more creative and empowering, enabling practitioners to challenge and change outmoded methods of working and ensuring their own clinical effectiveness'.

She adds that in such a model it is assumed that change evolves out of self-awareness, with the practitioner taking on much more the role of an action researcher than a passive consumer of knowledge. Reflective practice enables us to examine and evaluate current practice and identify what is being learnt, what ought to remain and what needs to change.

A more extensive discussion of reflective practice and how to undertake it is provided in *Chapter 5*, 'Reflection in professional development: personal experiences', by Nicola Spalding.

Reflective practice is best supported by a range of tools such as clinical reasoning, as discussed in *Chapter 3*, and critical incident analysis, which is the focus of this chapter. When used selectively, these strategies can help us reflect on experiences, identify learning outcomes and demonstrate our growth and professional development. It is suggested that where these tools are used regularly and when the process is documented, as in writing-up a critical incident, we are able to build up a portfolio of evidence demonstrating professional development.

Critical incidents

When we are asked to reflect on critical incidents, most of us are likely to raise the following questions:
- What is it?
- How do we do it?
- What do we do with it?

These are normal responses, as reflection is a difficult task to do without support (John, 1994).

According to Lillyman and Evans (1996), critical incidents are those that have made some emotional impact on us. The incident may be a positive or a negative experience. Benner (1984) suggests that critical incidents range from incidents that are ordinary and typical, to those that went unusually well or those that were particularly demanding.

Holm and Stephenson (1994) point out that there are no firm rules on the best way to reflect on one's practice, but with experience we are gradually able to build-up our own framework.

However, a list of questions acts as a useful guide to help us focus our thinking on critical incidents. For example, Cross (1997) asks us to consider four questions:

- What is the critical incident?
- What did I learn?
- How did I acquire the learning?
- How have I applied this learning in my practice?

A personal communication from Coles (in Alsop, 1995) suggests:

- What was the nature of the experience or event?
- What aspects of the event went well, or what was good about the experience?
- What did not go so well or was not so good?
- What were my feelings about what happened?
- What were the feelings of others?
- What have I learnt from the experience?
- What did others think I should learn?
- What do I need to do next?
- How can I use what I learnt in professional practice?

However, we must avoid reducing one's experiences to merely answering a series of questions 'that splinters the human encounter' (John, 1994). The questions should be used as an *aide memoire* to structure our experience in a meaningful way, as described by Cross (1997).

Professional development

'Professional development' is one of the modules that is offered to final-year occupational therapy and physiotherapy students at the School of Occupational Therapy and Physiotherapy, University of East Anglia.

Each student pursues three modules. Among the principal

intentions of the modules are to prepare students for reflective practice and make them aware that all the activity they undertake to enhance their knowledge and skills form a valid part of their development. Learning should take place throughout their career in response to CPD — a balance between formal learning (ie. completing post-qualification courses or attendance at conferences) and informal learning (which may include reflecting on practice and reading papers from journals).

Case study

The following case study is an account by a final-year occupational therapy student, who has identified among her needs to become more confident in practice; a commentary on the reflective aspect is given in italics.

Case study

"I chose to study 'Children with special needs' as one of the three modules. Initially, I found the process of reflection very difficult."

(*This statement suggests the initial frustration and anxiety among many students about the process of reflection.*)

"In the 4-week period before my placement, I had found the seminars on 'Children with special needs' quite frustrating. All of my colleagues except for one had been on paediatric placements, and I certainly felt a bit left out. Although the actual content of the seminars was appropriate for all of us, I felt I was unable to contribute to discussions because I lacked the experience that the others seemed to draw upon. So when I had the opportunity of having an 8-week paediatric placement, I was thrilled — but apprehensive at the same time. However, I had built-up an image that it would be enjoyable and rewarding to work with these lovely little children, and that it would be so different from working with an elderly client group."

(*This account indicates the student's acknowledgement of her lack of experience and her awareness of the need to use practice to support theoretical work.*)

"Throughout my first week I felt like a small fish in a very large pond. I was very much an observer, standing on the periphery of the groups that I attended. I was encouraged by my supervisors to just 'interact' with the children, but I could never have imagined how difficult this would be. I felt very inadequate watching the other staff interacting so well with them. I was surprised that I was so intimidated by the children....

I tried to speak with another little boy who was playing with some beads. I introduced myself, but he didn't even acknowledge my presence.... I left the session feeling totally defeated and a complete failure. I hadn't realized that communicating with children would be so different from normal conversation. For several days after this, my experiences in paediatric occupational therapy continued to be negative."

(*This account shows an honest reflection on the part of the student. It reminds practitioners not to assume that students can automatically undertake basic therapeutic skills such as interaction, be it working with children or older people.*)

"My confidence increased dramatically following an experience that I considered a critical incident at playgroup 2, when my supervisor asked me to carry out an occupational therapy assessment on a girl with cerebral palsy. I enjoyed the challenge that had been set, and it forced me to think on my feet as I put my knowledge into practice.

I instinctively used toys and games to assess the child's abilities, and it suddenly occurred to me that this is the role of occupational therapy in paediatrics; occupational therapists select specific activities to promote the development of specific skills, and then continually assess the children's progress as they observe them playing. Although this seems obvious now, I was not really aware of this during my first couple of weeks as I was concentrating on being used to being among children.

I feel that I have grown in confidence immensely since the incident. I gradually began to take on more of a role in planning and running activities, some of which went well and others not so well.... After only 8 weeks I cannot claim to understand all that there is to know about paediatric occupational therapy. However, I feel that by reflecting on the experiences that I have had on this placement, I have a better understanding of occupational therapy and have begun to develop the skills that are needed to address the unique problems of each individual child."

(*The above account shows that by being able to identify the critical incident, the student is able to identify her learning. She is also able to link theory and practice through the critical incident, which is many times more meaningful than being told about it or reading about it in textbooks.*)

"The professional development module has given me the opportunity to explore my learning process. I have learnt a variety of things about my personality and my preferred styles of learning that will help me to continue the learning process once I qualify.

With practice, reflection has begun to play a more and more important part in both my personal and professional developments. I find that I am able to learn best when I can identify a critical incident, which I can then go and investigate in the literature. I can then relate this knowledge back to practice, and the reflective cycle of learning begins.

This process of discovery through action increases my interest and my motivation to learn because I can amalgamate theory and practice in the context of the situation. I can continue this pattern of learning when I am a basic grade by reading and discussing books and journals, in order to increase and update my theoretical knowledge. I would also grasp every opportunity to attend relevant courses and workshops. Also, I shall continue to keep a reflective journal, as I have found this particularly useful on this placement. It will encourage me to think more about what I am doing, challenge practice, and become more competent.

I think that the final important thing that I have learnt throughout this module is that confidence is synonymous with knowledge and understanding. I feel that my confidence has increased so much because I have taken every opportunity to learn new skills and acquire new knowledge. I also have gained a deeper understanding of myself and the practice of occupational therapy through the process of reflection. As I approach the next stage in my career, I realize that my journey of discovery and development has only just begun."

(*The above accounts demonstrate a meaningful, reflective journey for the student. Through the reflection of the critical incident, a process of analysis and critical thinking has emerged, which has enabled her to learn from what she may initially have considered as an unsatisfactory fieldwork experience. This is a clear demonstration of a satisfactory level of reflection that has developed through a combination of self-awareness and regular practice to document experiences.*)

Conclusions

Critical incidents may be used as part of a personal portfolio/profile. They can be used to explore the links between theory and practice, and provide strategies for coping with similar incidents in the future. Without documenting the incident, it may be lost from memory with no evidence of learning or development. Furthermore, writing can provide an objectivity in relation to the initial learning experience (Walker, 1985). Finally, Holm and Stephenson (1994) maintain that reflection has assisted them to become more aware of the need to question the validity of their own and other's actions in relation to practice:

> *'Reflection enables us to find clarity and conclusion in the midst of confusion and conflict.'*

References

Alsop A (1995) The professional portfolio — purpose, process and practice. Part 2. *Br J Occup Ther* **58**: 337–40

Benner P (1984) *From Novice to Expert: Excellence and Power in Clinical Nursing Practice*. Addison Wesley, California

Boyd E, Fales A (1983) Reflecting learning: key to learning from experience. *J Humanistic Psychol* **23**: 99–117

Cross V (1997) The professional development diary — a case study of one cohort of physiotherapy students. *Physiotherapy* **83**: 375–83

Gibbs G (1988) *Learning by Doing*. FEU, London

Holm D, Stephenson S (1994) Reflection — a student's perspective. In: Palmer A, Burns S, Bulman C, eds. *Reflective Practice in Nursing*. Blackwell Science, Oxford: 53–62

John C (1994) Guided reflection. In: Palmer A, Burns S, Bulman C, eds. *Reflective Practice in Nursing*. Blackwell Science, Oxford: 110–29

Lillyman S, Evans, B (1996) *Designing a Personal Portfolio Profile: a Workbook for Healthcare Professionals*. Quay Books, Dinton

Walker D (1985) Writing and reflection. In: Boud R, Keogh R, Walker D, eds. *Reflection: Turning Experience into Learning*. Kogan Page, London: 63

Key points

❋ Reflective practice enables us to examine and evaluate current practice and identify what is being learnt, what ought to remain and what needs to change.

❋ Reflective practice is best supported by a range of tools such as clinical reasoning and critical incident analysis. When used selectively, these strategies can help us reflect on experiences, identify learning outcomes and demonstrate our growth and professional development.

❋ Critical incidents are those that have made some emotional impact on us. The incident may be a positive or a negative experience.

❋ Critical incidents may be used as part of a personal portfolio/profile. They can be used to explore the links between theory and practice, and provide strategies for coping with similar incidents in the future.

❋ Without documenting the incident, it may be lost from memory with no evidence of learning or development. Furthermore, writing can provide an objectivity in relation to the initial learning experience.

5

Reflection in professional development: personal experiences

Nicola Spalding

This chapter is based on the workshop 'Reflection' run by the author. The purpose of the workshop was to improve the therapists' understanding of reflection and to encourage its use. Here the theme is continued, and the theoretical discussion is integrated with two practical personal experiences. It is hoped that these experiences will serve those who are unfamiliar with reflection and its process, so that they might use the same or similar methods in their own practice situations.

Reflection

The immensity of the topic of reflection is evident from the literature. This is because reflection has been recognized as a tool for the specific purpose of continuing professional development (CPD) (Castle, 1996; Routledge *et al*, 1997; Stewart, 1998). CPD is now a requirement for all healthcare professionals. For example, the College of Occupational Therapists makes this clear in their position statement on lifelong learning (College of Occupational Therapists, 2002). Among the literature, however, the term 'reflection' still has various definitions and different accounts for the process, which might be confusing. Rather than add to these debates, the intention of this chapter is to demonstrate, with two case studies, how reflection has been used to improve practice. The hope is that it will clarify the process and motivate those who have not yet experienced its value.

What is reflection?

Reflection is about learning from experience. Quite simply, reflection can be 'thoughtful deliberation' (Tickle, 1994). Champion's (1991) more comprehensive explanation is that reflection is a process of examining and exploring issues in an attempt to improve and shape activities. Any situation, positive or negative, can be reflected upon for the purpose of learning — the outcome being a changed perspective.

> *'Reflective practice can take place on a formal or informal basis anytime one or more persons begin a process of inquiry for the purpose of examining actions and events as a means to understand and improve performance' (Osterman and Kottkamp, 1993).*

Reflection is a process-based learning activity (Stewart, 1998), which is self-directing and thus purposeful to the learner.

Reflective skills

An informative and coherent analysis of the literature by Atkins and Murphy (1993) revealed certain cognitive and affective skills required of the reflective practitioner, namely the ability to:

- *Be self-aware* — this enables a person to honestly analyse his or her feelings

- *Be descriptive* — a comprehensive account of the situation is detailed from a recollection of the event and experience
- *Critically analyse* — the examination of all the elements to the situation, such as existing knowledge, assumptions and possible alternatives; the 'So what?' questions
- *Synthesize ideas* — the incorporation of previous knowledge with newly acquired knowledge to give a new perspective to the situation
- *Evaluate* — also to give the new perspective, this is the assessment or appraisal of the situation from which judgments of worth can be made.

Schon (1991) also advocates that a reflective practitioner requires intuition. Although these skills have been identified, from my experience I found they could be developed while reflecting, and so should not be seen as necessary before attempting to reflect. I found that certain tools, to be discussed below, enabled me to develop and improve such skills.

The stages in the reflective process include the following:
1. Learning opportunity
2. Information-gathering and critical analysis
3. Changed perspective.

I shall use two personal experiences of reflection to illustrate these stages of the process.

Personal experience 1

Earlier in my teaching career I recognized a personal need to develop and improve my teaching skills. I wanted to equip myself with what I perceived I lacked in terms of practice and theory as a result of not having a teaching qualification.

'Learning to teach involves the development of technical skills as well as an appreciation of moral issues involved in education, an ability to negotiate and develop one's practice within the culture of the school, and an ability to reflect and evaluate in and on one's actions' (Calderhead, 1991, p.531).

Schon (1991) suggests that reflection is most likely initiated when a professional is dissatisfied with their performance. I therefore decided to carry out an evaluation of my abilities, and make improvements in light of the evaluation. This is the first stage in the reflective process, which Boyd and Fales (1983) refer to as a sense of inner discomfort. For me it was the impetus for self-evaluation and improvement.

Another tool to help identify learning goals might result from a personal 'strengths, weaknesses, opportunities and threats' (SWOT) analysis (Atkinson, 1998). My learning opportunities were each of my teaching sessions.

The second stage of the reflective process is one of information-gathering and critical analysis. This is an examination of feelings and knowledge, which is seen as constructive development. To evaluate myself I video-recorded some of my teaching sessions and kept a reflective diary. The diary was used after every lesson in which I taught. Thorpe (1993) suggests that writing is a way of capturing thoughts and feelings and of structuring and using reflection strategically for intentional learning. First, I described the practice situation. Second, to analyse the experience I answered the following questions:

- What did I feel both during and after the situation?
- What was positive about the situation and why?
- What felt less positive and why?
- What were my reasons for my practice?
- What would I do differently next time in light of this analysis?
- What did I learn from the situation?

If I discussed the situation with colleagues afterwards, I also documented their response and suggestions, followed by my thoughts on what they said, thus considering a range of perspectives (Fish et al, 1991). The video-recordings were viewed and written-up in the same way.

Justifying actions and consideration of the theoretical basis for these encourages the analytical process. It was important to state why I behaved in a certain way. I could then refer to the literature on teaching to increase my theoretical knowledge and consider ideas and theories for improvement in practice. From the descriptive data, analysis then needs to be encouraged. Fish et al (1991) state that this is:

'...concerned with discovering and exploring the assumptions, beliefs and value judgments that underlie the events and the ideas which emerge...and does not merely involve superficial criticism of what happened in practice' (p.27).

The question 'What would I do differently next time in light of this analysis?' was the most useful for me in the whole reflective process because it moved me forward.

For example, one of my critical incidents was a teaching session, 'wheelchair prescription', which was in a cramped room. In my diary I noted the cramped conditions that compromised safety and limited the use of audiovisual aids. At the same time, I also felt disappointed by the lack of student participation in the various activities incorporated into the lesson. My conclusion was that the room I had used was obviously too small in this instance, and my reasons for using it were only because that was what had been previously used by another lecturer. I considered the poor student interactions and thought that a larger room, enabling the students to sit in a circle, would facilitate better discussions. This was reinforced in the literature, which advocated a circle for encouraging student participation (Locke and Ciechalski, 1995).

Having answered the analysis question I then planned a repeat lesson as though I was going to teach it again. In this example it included booking a different, larger room, having considered the equipment I wanted to use and the circled seating arrangement on my lesson plan. Keeping a record of all these events enabled me to focus my ideas for improvement. The following year when I was planning my timetable I was able to apply the reflections from my diary. Alsop (1995) argues the importance of systematic documentation for ease of clarification and future reference.

From this analysis I was able to realise my learning, which was the significance of seating arrangements depending on the lesson purpose, the incorporation of all the teaching aids and the importance of planning accordingly. This is the final stage in the reflective process, the learning or outcome of reflection. Boud et al (1985) see this as resulting in both affective and cognitive changes, which may lead to behavioural changes. This is the new outlook on the situation — the changed perspective.

The descriptive diary entries after the lesson also made it apparent how much had gone on during the session. There seemed to be so much material to reflect upon. I believe that some of this information retrieved by this documentation process would have been otherwise forgotten, and therefore not used for reflecting upon. For me committing the experience into a written form stimulated my memory, allowing me to reflect in more detail. Answering the questions then gave me structure to the process and kept me focused.

Personal experience 2

Practising reflection in a group has been recognized as beneficial for group members to support each other and promote better understanding than might be achieved alone (Barnett, 1994). My second personal experience provides evidence of the value of group reflection.

As part of a large case study, I was involved in an action research project with a multidisciplinary group of healthcare professionals. The purpose was to improve their preoperative education programme that they provided for patients awaiting a total hip replacement. This research provided a learning opportunity for the healthcare professionals who had not previously met together to discuss their service or evaluate its effectiveness.

A number of evaluative methods of data collection were used, including patient questionnaires, patient interviews, interviews with the healthcare professionals and individual written reflections using the questions listed above in personal experience 1. Team meetings were then instigated within the action research process to discuss this evaluative data. In these meetings, group reflections were seen to evolve. The healthcare professionals worked together to critically analyse the data. They would ask each other questions and debate issues that arose, thus encouraging critical analysis from the data.

As one of the healthcare professionals stated:

'Discussion could take place on what we were doing well and what could be improved upon.'

The meetings were seen as legitimate time to reflect for the purpose of improving. This reflection enabled the healthcare professionals to work together on a shared purpose, something the service previously lacked. It also enabled the healthcare professionals the opportunity to give constructive feedback to each other and advance their previous individual reflections of the service.

As one healthcare professional stated:

'It gave us time to think more about what we were doing to plan for the next one. I would have reflected, but not probably as much...and you hear what others have to say too, which makes you think more.'

As a consequence of the reflections and discussions in the meetings, the healthcare professionals learnt a great deal about both the preoperative educational product and the preoperative educational process. They had a changed perspective, which resulted in 21 direct changes to the programme. The healthcare professionals viewed these changes as substantial service improvements.

Overcoming hindrances to reflection

It may be that reflecting on one's practices is seen as another chore in an already busy day, and that it has a low priority compared with other duties. My experiences were, however, that it improved practice a great deal and was therefore worth the time invested in it. Further justification is provided from professional bodies who make CPD a requirement for the regulation of quality assurance in healthcare. For example, the College of Occupational Therapists (2002, p.198) says:

> *'Occupational therapy personnel have a responsibility to use new technologies and new learning in order to maximize their impact for the benefit of service users and their carers.'*

Reflection could be from this 'new learning'.

Efficiency is often a goal for all of us, and is encouraged by our managers. However, efficiency often means a task becomes routine, and a routine is harder to reflect upon. It is difficult to analyse and question because the task is so automatic. The efficient therapist might therefore find some initial difficulty. However, reflection, like any new skill, requires practice in order that it becomes refined. Through practice I also learnt to be more analytical. The questions were useful here by breaking down the task into stages, and they reminded me to analyse and move forward.

An alternative to writing-up experiences is the verbalization of an event. An experienced other can act as a mentor to encourage the reflection process by asking the questions and ensuring there is an answer. As Plato stated:

> *'A wise man learns from experience, and an even wiser man from the experience of others.'*

This further justifies group reflections.

As with any new skill it is advisable to make an easy start. Being overambitious might set you up for failure, and the demoralising effect of such failure will be memorable and serve to deter you from repeating the process.

The final factor to consider is that of motivation. Being motivated will help commitment. This can be achieved in part by understanding the reasons for reflecting, ie. the belief in improvement. I also felt motivated from the learning that took place, thus encouraging me to continue. One should acknowledge the rewards as they arise.

Evidence

When presented at first, the theory of reflection may serve to daunt the professional who wishes to learn from practice. However, on closer review the skills required are evident in our daily practice. These skills, so fundamental to therapists, are likely to have been developed during our professional training. Most of us regularly evaluate our interventions and interactions with clients and colleagues. We frequently change our treatment regimen because we have noted no improvement. To do this we obviously engaged to some extent in the reflective process. To make it really reflective, however, we then need to learn from the situation, the learning of which will then inform our future practice.

Further justification for practitioners to document their reflections and subsequent learning is provided when others require evidence of our CPD. This might be for purposes of supervision, mentoring, personal development plans or appraisal interviews. Extracts from a reflective diary may be such evidence. The shift then for some practitioners may just be one of documentation of the subsequent learning.

Conclusions

It is hoped that the case studies presented will serve those who are unfamiliar with reflection and its process, so that they might use the same or similar methods in their own practice situations. There are no prescriptions on what tools should be used, rather whatever people feel aids them to reflect on their practice situations. These might include diaries, illustrations, a set of questions, a mentor or a group of supportive colleagues. The investment and commitment to learning the art of reflection will result in reward. That is, it maximizes the learning potential from many practice situations, and thus aids one's CPD.

References

Alsop A (1995) The professional portfolio — purpose, process and practice. Part 2: producing a portfolio from experiential learning. *Br J Occup Ther* **58**: 337–40

Atkins S, Murphy K (1993) Reflection: a review of the literature. *J Adv Nurs* **18**: 1188–92

Atkinson K (1998) SWOT analysis: a tool for continuing professional development. *Br J Ther Rehabil* **5**(8): 433–5

Barnett R (1994) *The Limits of Competence: Knowledge, Higher Education and Society*. Society for Research into Higher Education and Open University Press, Buckenham

Boud D, Keogh R, Walker D (1985) *Reflection: Turning Experience into Learning*. Kegan Page, London

Boyd E, Fales A (1983) Reflective learning: key to learning from experience. *J Human Psychol* **23**(2): 99–117

Calderhead J (1991) The nature and growth of knowledge in student teaching. *Teach Teacher Educ* **7**: 531–5

Castle A (1996) Developing the ethos of reflective practice for continuing professional development. *Br J Ther Rehabil* **3**(7): 358–9

Champion R (1991) Educational accountability: what do the 1990s? *Nurs Educ Today* **11**: 407–19

College of Occupational Therapists (2002) College of Occupational Therapists: position statement on lifelong learning. *Br J Occup Ther* **65**(5): 198–200

Fish D, Twinn S, Purr B (1991) Promoting reflection: improving the supervision of practice in health visiting and initial teacher training. In: *How to Enable Students to Learn Through Professional Practice*. Report 2. West London Institute of Higher Education, Middlesex

Locke D, Ciechalski C (1995) *Psychological Techniques for Teachers*. 2nd edn. Accelerated Development, Washington DC

Osterman K, Kottkamp R (1993) *Reflective Practice for Educators: Improving Schooling Through Professional Development*. Corwin Press, California

Routledge J, Willson M, McArthur M, Richardson B, Stephenson R (1997) Reflection on the development of a reflective assessment. *Med Teacher* **19**(2): 122–8

Schon D (1991) *The Reflective Practitioner: How Professionals Think in Action*. 2nd edn. Jossey Bass, San Francisco

Stewart S (1998) The place of portfolios within continuing professional development. *Br J Ther Rehabil* **5**(5): 266–9

Thorpe M (1993) Experiential learning at a distance. In: Boud D, Cohen R, Walker D, eds. *Using Experience for Learning*. Society for Research in Higher Education and Open University Press, Buckenham

Tickle L (1994) *The Induction of New Teachers*. Cassell, London

Further reading

Cross V (1993) Introducing physiotherapy students to the idea of reflective practice. *Med Teacher* **15**(4): 293–307

Parham D (1987) Toward professionalism: the reflective therapist. *Am J Occup Ther* **41**(9): 555–60

Key points

⌘ Reflective practice has been recognized for its potential in CPD.

⌘ Reflection is a process-based learning activity, which is self-directing and thus purposeful to the learner.

⌘ The reflective practitioner will be required to be self-aware, descriptive, analytical, evaluative and be able to synthesize ideas.

⌘ Three stages in the reflection process can be identified, namely the impetus for change, the critical analysis and the learning outcome.

⌘ Personal strategies can be used to aid the reflection process, such as illustrations and questions.

⌘ There are possible barriers that can hinder the reflection process, so a further challenge exists to overcome them.

⌘ The final factor to consider is that of motivation. Being motivated will help commitment. This can be achieved in part by understanding the reasons for reflecting, i.e. the belief in improvement.

⌘ The documentation of the learning as a consequence of reflection may be used as evidence of one's CPD.

6

SWOT analysis: a tool for CPD

Kim Atkinson

Continuing professional development (CPD) is high on the agenda for all professionals working in health and social care. This chapter suggests desirable qualities for an individual wishing to engage in CPD. It goes on to outline how SWOT (strengths, weaknesses, opportunities and threats) analysis can be applied as a tool to help facilitate the progression of CPD. An illustration of the use of SWOT analysis in a professional development exercise is given, which facilitates the establishment of priorities, action plans and strategies for future development.

Introduction

Continuing professional development (CPD) is high on the agenda for all professionals working in health and social care, in particular those in the professions supplementary to medicine who are anticipating the reform to the Professions Supplementary to Medicine Act 1960. Much debate has taken place at local, regional and national levels about what form CPD should take, and how it might be meaningfully directed.

Integral to this has been the production of packages, often based on a portfolio design, to help direct and record individual

CPD. Two examples of such packages are the Chartered Society of Physiotherapy's *Professional Development Diary* (1994) and the College of Occupational Therapists' *Professional Development Programme* (1996), both of which are based on a portfolio design.

Qualities for CPD

The College of Occupational Therapists (1996) states that individuals wishing to engage in CPD need to have:

- Objectives for learning based on a clear understanding of their personal capabilities, career goals and professional aspirations
- A systematic approach to CPD in order to have the best chance of being successful
- A clear understanding of their current situation.

While the College of Occupational Therapists (1996) also states that CPD is an attitude and not a technique, it is evident that the use of techniques and tools is likely to help the individual achieve the above three qualities. This chapter outlines how a SWOT (strengths, weaknesses, opportunities and threats) analysis can be used as a tool to facilitate CPD activities.

SWOT analysis

SWOT analysis has been widely adopted as a marketing tool where it is used as a way of analysing the features of a given situation in terms of strengths, weaknesses, opportunities and threats. From this, priorities, goals and strategies for change can be identified (NHS Training Directorate, 1991; Jones and McDonnell, 1993). In addition, it is often appropriate in the SWOT analysis to give some consideration to timescales (Smyth, 1996). Just as a SWOT analysis is useful for facilitating the development of this process in marketing, it can also be applied to CPD in helping the individual achieve the desirable qualities for CPD, as identified above.

In a practical sense, a SWOT analysis is completed simply by dividing a page into four and considering what should be included under each heading (*Figure 6.1*).

Strengths	Weaknesses
Opportunities	Threats

Figure 6.1. Usual layout for SWOT (strengths, weaknesses, opportunities and threats) analysis.

Identifying SWOT components

Strengths and weaknesses usually refer to the analysis of the individual, and opportunities and threats to the analysis of the external environment (NHS Training Directorate, 1991). Thus, in relation to CPD, a SWOT analysis can be used to help the individual to consider his or her own personal strengths and weaknesses against the backdrop of external opportunities and threats. This is important because no individual operates in isolation, and the demands and priorities of the work situation as well as issues in personal life will all impact significantly on CPD options and priorities.

In completing a SWOT analysis it becomes evident that many features will have both positive and negative aspects to them (NHS Training Directorate, 1991), and this should be acknowledged and analysed in the process.

Once the SWOT analysis is complete, the aim is to:

- Build on strengths
- Turn weaknesses into strengths
- Make the most of opportunities
- Plan around threats (NHS Training Directorate, 1991).

This is achieved through the development of action plans and strategies.

Fulfilling the aims of SWOT analysis

At this point an illustration of a SWOT analysis used to address a professional development issue might be useful. At the School of Occupational Therapy and Physiotherapy, University of East Anglia, the first piece of assessed work that undergraduate students are asked to complete is a SWOT analysis of their personal and professional strengths in relation to the demands of the undergraduate programme. *Figure 6.2* is an example of a completed SWOT analysis.

The process of thinking through a situation and writing down features in a structured manner helps to crystallize and formalize the thoughts and feelings of what is often a multi-

Strengths	**Weaknesses**
Worked as an occupational therapist helper	Didn't do A-level biology
Lots of practice in essay writing	Hate presenting
Work professionally as a singer	Tend not to speak up because of lack of confidence
Good at getting on with people	Get anxious about abilities, especially when uncertain of what is expected
Adaptable, flexible	
Enthusiastic	Didn't know about academic writing
Good at thinking around issues	
	No computer skills
Opportunities	**Threats**
To be here: a chance to be an occupational therapist	Working as a singer
	Not knowing what is expected
Chance to develop own skills at finding out information	Rather enjoying social life at university
Placements	Lack of money
Dissection	Dissection
A chance to be at university, with all that it entails	Work as an occupational therapist helper

Figure 6.2. Example of a completed SWOT (strengths, weaknesses, opportunities and threats) analysis.

faceted situation. For example, in the SWOT analysis in *Figure 6.2,* the student identified that having worked as an occupational therapy helper was viewed as both a strength and a threat. The student perceived it as a strength because it meant starting the course with some prior knowledge and understanding of the work of the occupational therapist in a particular clinical area. However, it was also perceived as a threat because of concern that others, particularly fieldwork educators and other students in the peer group, would assume that the student had more knowledge and expertise than was the reality. Having completed the SWOT analysis, the student is helped to identify the priorities that need to be worked on, and to select tools and strategies that might help achieve the student's goals.

Individual or team activity

The SWOT analysis and subsequent action planning can be completed either as an individual and personal exercise, perhaps in preparation for an annual appraisal exercise, or as a team activity to identify CPD requirements in light of the changes or demands the team might be facing.

As with all tools, SWOT analysis has its limitations; it only takes the individual part of the way down the route of CPD. Having helped individuals to analyse their current situation, they still have to be sufficiently reflective and analytical to identify and set their priorities, goals and strategies for change, and to evaluate how these might be achieved within their current situation.

Conclusions

Although widely used as a marketing tool, SWOT analysis can be applied to a variety of situations, including the analysis of CPD needs through helping individuals or teams to analyse their current situation in a structured manner. This can then facilitate the establishment of priorities, action plans and strategies for future development.

References

Chartered Society of Physiotherapy (1994) *Professional Development Diary*. Chartered Society of Physiotherapy, London

College of Occupational Therapists (1996) *Professional Development Programme*. College of Occupational Therapists, London

Jones A, McDonnell U (1993) *Managing The Clinical Resource: An Action Guide for Health Professionals*. Ballière Tindall, London

NHS Training Directorate (1991) *Health Pick Up — Marketing Your Services*. Presentation Pack 982170. Intek Europe Ltd, Hove

Smyth T (1996) *Managing Health and Social Care*. Macmillan, London

Key points

✽ Engaging in CPD requires the individual to adopt a systematic approach and to have a clear understanding of his or her current situation.

✽ SWOT (strengths, weaknesses, opportunities and threats) analysis is a credible tool for facilitating CPD.

✽ SWOT analysis helps the individual consider his or her personal strengths and weaknesses against the backdrop of external opportunities and threats.

✽ SWOT analysis serves as a springboard for action-planning by establishing priorities, goals and strategies for CPD.

7

Information management and technology: a vital part of CPD?

Robin Shutt, Rod Lambert

This chapter explores the origins and proposed function of the NHS 'Information Strategy for the Modern NHS' in its initial and continuing format. It then considers five perspectives on how information management and technology (IM&T) can and should be used within plans for continuing professional development (CPD). The perspectives are: update on current technology; IM&T to inform practice; IM&T to inform planning; analysis of present practice; and IM&T to inform management decisions. The chapter concludes that the inclusion of IM&T within individual plans for CPD can enhance our ability to play a major role in our own professional development, the future of our professions and the NHS as a whole.

Introduction

In June 1996, the NHS Executive published an information leaflet entitled *Establishing NHSnet* (NHS Executive, 1996a). It begins by citing an extract from a report on the 'burdens of paperwork', which states:

> *'The potential for information technology to reduce paperwork in interactions between NHS organizations has touched every part of our scrutiny. When NHS organizations are able to communicate electronically, there will be enormous improvements in efficiency and significant gains for patient care' (NHS Executive, 1996a).*

This claim is one which would be welcomed by all, but the reality often seems a long way off. The NHS information management and technology (IM&T) strategy has evolved into the 'information for health' strategy 1998, which is part of a governmental drive to increase access to all relevant information. This *Information Strategy for the Modern NHS* builds on the concepts initially set out by the NHS Information Management Group (IMG) and has implemented many of the proposals. The following shows what has been achieved so far (NHSIA, 1998):

- NHS Direct covers the whole of England
- Improved access to information on health, conditions and treatment
- Improved access to knowledge and evidence bases
- Connecting GP practices to *NHSnet*
- Improving patient care through wider use of electronic records
- Improved funding for information technology
- Developing local information strategies

The IM&T infrastructure

The IM&T infrastructure depends on ensuring that there is adherence to standards. These standards will allow all parts of the NHS to continue and develop the connections that lead to improving access to information about patients and populations, and to more efficient contracting. This infrastructure enables the NHS to maximize the potential that both information management and the associated technology offer.

The following projects have an impact on all NHS organizations.

1. Adhering to standards:
- National data and information technology standards
- National electronic messages
- Security and confidentiality
- GP system accreditation.

2. More efficient contracting:
- NHS-wide clearing service
- Contract minimum data set
- Healthcare resource groups.

3. Making the connections:
- NHS-wide networking
- Family Health Service Authority/GP electronic links.

4. Better information about patients and populations:
- Replacement NHS number
- International Classification of Diseases (ICD-10; World Health Organization, 1994) implementation
- NHS administrative registers.

So, with a commitment towards such a strategy, where does our individual continuing professional development (CPD) fit within it?

We would like to suggest that the potential benefits of the IM&T strategy are vast. But, as therapists, we will only be able to make use of those benefits if we use CPD to update knowledge. We suggest, therefore, that there are five main areas where CPD should be considered as a realistic and vital link between the theory and practice; these can be seen in *Figure 7.1.*

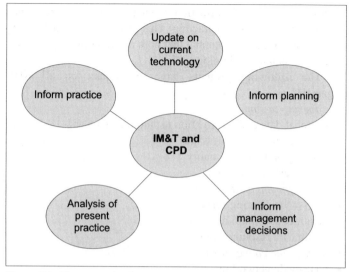

Figure 7.1. Elements of information management and training (IM&T) that link to CPD.

Update on current technology

It is a fact of life that as techniques and equipment change we have to update our knowledge to remain effective. This point was well illustrated by McBain and Renton (1997) in an article about computer-assisted cognitive rehabilitation, where they stated that therapists continued to use '10-year-old programs on 13-year-old technology'.

The technology is, admittedly, constantly developing, and it sometimes feels as if current purchases are obsolete before they arrive in a department. However, the development of the electronic patient record (NHS Executive, 1996b) as part of the IM&T strategy has led to specific criteria being established for all new hardware purchases. It is therefore important to understand the terminology and the technology behind it, to be able to make use of it. Such updating itself can and should form part of CPD.

Having developed knowledge of the technology, it cannot be allowed to stop at that point. What is also required is a working, up-to-date knowledge of how the technology (both hardware and software) can be used within management and in clinical settings. It is beyond the scope of this chapter to enter into detailed discussion about specific items, but it would hardly make sense to have a computer in the department, linked to the rest of the hospital or to the rest of the Trust and through this to the whole of the NHS, and not know how to access the wealth of information available.

This again requires access to appropriate training, so that both clinical and management applications can be explored in detail. The information can then be accessed more confidently, and can then be used in an effective manner. This leads on to the second area for CPD.

IM&T to inform practice

Let us assume for a moment that the *NHSnet* is available to all. This means that we have access to all our own patient information, and to the major aspects of other units' treatments and outcomes. At present, when we are left with questions about the efficacy of our treatment processes, we can audit them and look at what our outcomes are, relative to a previous time. We can also look at what other units are doing through published articles.

The value of the information we now have access to is that we can make a direct comparison between our own intervention and its outcome with that of other units throughout the UK. The information is not dependent upon lead times between studies and the publication of their results; it is contemporary information that is constantly updated.

The use of such data, for example by the National Institute of Clinical Excellence (NICE), is then invaluable in considering whether the chosen treatment is the most effective. Where other units are obtaining better outcomes, it offers the opportunity to discover more about the methods being used, leading in some cases to changes in practice at local level. The use of information in this way is only possible if the knowledge has been updated through a process of CPD that considers IM&T an important feature and a functional tool.

An additional element of the use of IM&T to inform practice is that it is more likely to generate research into areas of specific need, or within specialties. As with the previous example, the access and interpretation of current data can help to identify areas where insufficient information is available; rather than leaving the investigation for somebody else to do, it now becomes possible to use the information available for research purposes.

Using IM&T to inform planning

One of the major criticisms of many information systems over the years has been that it has been a 'one-way street', because while information has been provided for 'managers', useful information being fed back to those providing it has been minimal. Continuing with the example of access to the *NHSnet*, the management information is intended to be removed 'transparently' from the databases, so that effort is directed towards the provision of clinical information that is based on current usage or need.

Patient information is the core of the system, along with treatment information and outcomes. Linked to this is human resource information and other information, making it possible to identify the costs linked to specific patient care. This can be at an individual level, for diagnostic groups of patients or for considering geographical areas.

Access to this information enables a service manager to identify a range of features about their service, where previously they relied on data provided from elsewhere (which was frequently considered to be inaccurate). Issues can now be considered, such as:

- The trend in attendance to specific areas
- Whether these trends are reflected in other specialties
- What impact has a change in staffing had on attendance and/or outcome?
- What gaps are there in provision, and what is required to fill them?

From access to information about these, and many other questions, it is possible to identify general and specific trends, and to play an increasingly active role in service planning.

Analysis of present practice

It is clear from the discussion so far that IM&T can play an important role in decision making at both a managerial and clinical level. We would like to focus now on the use of IM&T in the analysis of present practice. With ready access to information about our own clinical practice so that we can see patterns and identify outcomes, it is now easier to compare our own results with those from other units throughout the UK and form electronic 'lists' from a wider global community. Such a comparison and communication would previously have been extremely difficult. This information can then be used to either confirm that current practice compares favourably with that in other units from a range of perspectives (eg. duration of intervention, outcome, relapse rate, patient satisfaction, etc), or it can suggest that change to a more effective method of treatment may be advisable.

IM&T to inform management decisions

We have already discussed the use of information to inform planning, but we remain a part of a wider organization, the Trust, or at a wider level, the NHS. If we do not have access to information, or we do not understand or know how to use the information effectively, we can expect to have little influence on the planning process at a higher level.

In terms of resource allocation and the general strategic direction of the organization, if we can demonstrate the service contribution to meeting the objectives of the business plan, it is more likely that a service voice will be heard.

From the other direction, if we are able to access information about the strategic direction, and can act quickly to put a case for how the service can provide an effective contribution towards that direction, the case for additional resources may be heard more sympathetically than otherwise.

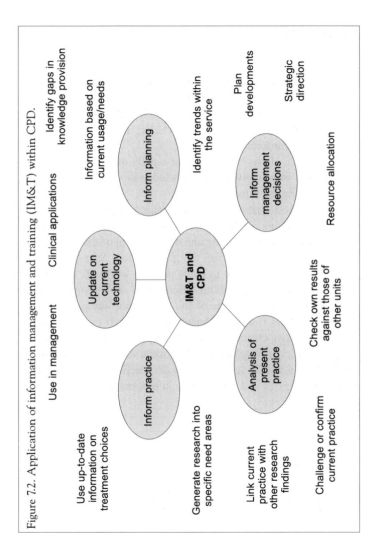

Figure 7.2. Application of information management and training (IM&T) within CPD.

Conclusions

We began by reviewing the NHS IM&T strategy, and have considered the possible ways in which this can impact on services. We have demonstrated ways in which CPD is vital in the development and updating of knowledge, involving technology and the use of information.

Figure 7.2 shows how the major aspects of the IM&T strategy can be used effectively, if the knowledge is available on how to access and use the information.

We suggest that CPD is an essential part of the equation relating to whether the therapy professions will continue to play an important part in the planning and development of the NHS for the millennium. Many parts of the *Information Strategy for the Modern NHS* are already in place and are working. We need to update our knowledge about information technology now, as evidenced by the adoption of the 'European computer driving licence' (ECDL) as the baseline standard of information technology competence, so that we can play a major role in our own professional development, the future of our professions and the NHS as a whole. It is from this perspective that we conclude that knowledge of and competence in practice in IM&T is a vital part of CPD.

References

McBain K, Renton LBM (1997) Computer-assisted cognitive rehabilitation and occupational therapy. *Br J Occup Ther* **60**: 199–204

NHS Executive (1995) *The Information Management and Technology Strategy for the NHS in England: An Updated Overview.* NHS Executive, Leeds

NHS Executive (1996a) *Establishing NHSnet.* NHS Executive, Leeds

NHS Executive (1996b) *The Facts About EPR: Electronic Patient Records.* NHS Executive, Leeds

NHSIA (1998) http://www.nhsia.nhs.uk/def/pages/info4health/1.asp

World Health Organization (1994) *International Statistical Classification of Diseases and Related Health Problems.* 10th revision (ICD–10). World Health Organization, Geneva

Key points

✱ The NHS Information Management and Technology (IM&T) strategy is a reality, and will influence our working practice.

✱ Planning to include IM&T within personal plans for CPD will assist in updating knowledge and promoting positive use of the available information and technology.

✱ Knowledge of IM&T can assist clinicians through informing practice, informing planning, analysing present practice and informing management decisions.

✱ The inclusion of IM&T within plans for CPD will enable individuals to play a full role in the future of professions and the NHS.

✱ IM&T is a vital part of CPD.

8

Learning contracts in practice: their role in continuing professional development

Elizabeth Walker

This chapter is based on a workshop run by the author, which considered the stages in designing learning contracts, their advantages and limitations, and the role of learning contracts in continuing professional development (CPD). For the purpose of this chapter, the term 'learner' is used to describe the person who carries out the contract, and the term 'mentor' describes the person who facilitates this process.

Introduction

Learning contracts are derived from the ideas of educators such as Malcolm Knowles, who believe that what adults choose to learn on their own initiative is learned more deeply and permanently than in 'traditional' education, where the learning process is structured primarily by the teacher and the institution (Knowles, 1990). Learning contracts are increasingly used in the professional development of the healthcare professions (Martenson and Schwab, 1993; Cross, 1996; Lowry, 1997); they facilitate learning in the 'real world' context of the learner (Quinn, 1988) and enable all those involved to be clear about the purpose, process and outcomes of the learning experience.

Learning contracts normally involve two parties, such as a student occupational therapist and his or her fieldwork educator, or a newly qualified clinician and his or her manager. In the literature, it is apparent that various terms are used to describe those involved. For the purpose of this chapter, the term 'learner' is used to describe the person who carries out the contract, and the term 'mentor' describes the person who facilitates this process.

What are learning contracts?

Learning contracts have been defined by several authors. Donald (1976) suggests that a learning contract is a document drawn up by a learner and mentor that:

> '...specifies what [the learner] will learn, how this will be accomplished, within what period of time, and what the criteria of evaluation will be.'

This definition, while useful, does not appear to acknowledge the aspect of flexibility that can be a major feature of learning contracts.

Tompkins and McGraw (1988) illustrate this by focusing more on the process of negotiation, and hence the relationship that exists between the learner and the mentor. They suggest that contracting is 'a continuously re-negotiable working agreement' between the learner and mentor, and emphasize that it is this process itself that encourages the skills for autonomous learning.

Brookfield (1996) suggests that learning contracts are 'the chief mechanism used as an enhancement of self-direction', thus enabling learners to control their learning experiences to meet their own needs and develop skills to educate themselves. It is this aspect and the fact that learning contracts can be used in a wide range of environments that makes them such a potentially useful tool in continuing professional development (CPD). However, Lowry (1997) points out that using learning contracts should not be seen as an easy option to remove pressure from the mentor, as there is still an important role for the mentor to play.

Developing a learning contract

There are a number of stages involved in developing a learning contract; the stages detailed in *Table 8.1* have been adapted from Anderson *et al* (1996).

Table 8.1. Stages involved in developing a learning contract
Identify a relevant learning need
Establish goals or objectives
Specify learning resources and strategies
Determine the evidence of accomplishment
State how the evidence will be validated, and criteria for assessment
Review the contract
Carry out the contract
Submission and self-assessment
From Anderson *et al* (1996)

Identify a relevant learning need

Initially the learner will need to establish his or her learning needs. Ideas may arise from numerous sources, such as lectures, courses, competency standards and discussions with peers. Learners may have difficulty in identifying their needs (Martens, 1981), especially if they are accustomed to more traditional teaching methods. Therefore, support from their mentor is particularly important at this stage in facilitating this process and in ensuring that the learners' perceived needs are appropriate for their stage of development.

Establish goals or objectives

In this stage, learning needs must be translated into precise statements that will serve to provide the focus for learning strategies. Goals or objectives may be concerned with acquisition or improvement of a skill, or may focus on increasing a student's knowledge of a particular topic. It is important that goals are specific, manageable and achievable for the resources and time available.

Learners tend to include too many objectives, often because of their erroneous belief that they should know absolutely everything about a topic. Mentors may need to emphasize to learners the importance of the quality of their learning, and not simply the quantity (McAllister, 1996). Time spent on this and on ensuring that the objectives are unambiguous will save time at a later date when evidence of achievement is sought.

Specify learning resources and strategies

Resources may include books and journals, professional associations, work colleagues, seminars and conferences, case notes, personal diaries, librarians and mentors. The learner may need support at this stage in identifying and accessing these if they are working in a new and unfamiliar environment. If the resources are not readily available, the benefits gained in their use may not be cost-effective (Lowry, 1997).

Discussion between mentor and learner is important at this stage to ensure that the learner's expectations are realistic (See 'Advantages and disadvantages of learning contracts', below).

Determine the evidence of accomplishment

In this stage, learners suggest one or more activities that will be used to convince themselves and others that their objectives have been achieved. These should be considered when the objectives are first formulated. Examples of completed evidence include:

- Demonstration
- Case studies
- Journal paper
- Essay
- Diary
- Clinical notes.

The evidence needs to be appropriate for the type of learning. For example: demonstration of a task-centred skill such as a manipulation technique; diary as evidence of development of reflective skills; and a literature review as evidence of critical appraisal.

State how the evidence will be validated, and criteria for assessment

The learner and mentor need to agree upon appropriate criteria for the objectives. This will vary depending on the type of objective; for example, an essay, case report or project presentation might be suitable evidence of understanding. Criteria for evaluation should be clearly stated to prevent ambiguity. The level that the learner has attained must be considered to ensure the criteria are appropriate. Thus, there may be occasions where the opinion of someone with specialist experience, who is not directly involved in the contract, is needed. This will need to be identified within the resources required for completion of the contract.

A learning contract form used in the School of Occupational Therapy and Physiotherapy, University of East Anglia, is shown in *Figure 8.1*.

Student		Supervisor	
Date agreed		Date due	
Learning goals	Strategies and resources	What is to be assessed	Evidence
Signature of student		Signature of supervisor	

Figure 8.1. Fieldwork learning contract, as used in the School of Occupational Therapy and Physiotherapy, University of East Anglia.

Review the contract

A period of reflection (usually about a week) is useful at this stage. The learner can review the contract either individually to see if it matches the original intention(s), or with colleagues who may offer a new perspective. The list below could be used as a checklist, maybe in discussion with peers and/or an adviser (Knowles, 1990):

- Are the goals or objectives clear, understandable, realistic and achievable?
- Are there other strategies or resources that might be considered?
- Does the evidence seem relevant and appropriate to the various objectives or intentions, and is it convincing?
- Is there other evidence that might be considered?
- Are the criteria and means for validating the evidence clear and relevant?

Carry out the contract

The time taken to carry out the contract depends on the goals and objectives that have been set, and needs to be negotiated between the learner and his or her mentor. The timescale needs to be realistic so as to make accomplishment of the goals and objectives possible for the learner to achieve; this could be anything from a couple of weeks to 6 months or longer. The amount of ongoing supervision will vary, depending on the learner's needs. It is important to note that changes can still be made at this stage in consultation with the adviser.

Submission and self-assessment

Here the contract may be used as a checklist by the learner. For example: 'Have the stated goals been met?' 'Is the evidence suitable?'

This will encourage the learner to take responsibility for the learning they have undertaken.

Advantages and disadvantages of learning contracts

Anderson *et al* (1996) list the following advantages of learning contracts:

- They are individual to the learner, therefore increase motivation
- They are flexible, thus can be tailored to suit the individual's learning style and pace of learning
- They encourage self-directed learning
- They bring a sense of ownership to the learner's activities and to the learning process.

Dart and Clarke (1991) add that learning contracts encourage a deep approach to learning, thus facilitating understanding of knowledge rather than taking a surface approach that promotes rote learning.

Learning contracts may therefore be a useful tool for CPD and could be included in a portfolio. However, learners who are new to the process of learning contracts may find the initial flexibility of learning contracts stressful, especially if they are accustomed to a learning environment that is didactic in nature, where the student has a more passive role. Staff who become mentors may need to attend workshops to familiarize themselves with the process of implementing learning contracts and to discuss their roles, especially if they themselves are accustomed to 'traditional' education.

The word 'contract' was identified by clinical educators as an area of concern at a workshop session on implementing learning contracts at a fieldwork educators' conference a few years ago. It is important to emphasize the process of negotiation, which should occur between the mentor and the learner. This could also alleviate another concern voiced by both educators and participants in the workshop at the CPD conference, namely that the learners would have unduly high expectations of resources, which might not be available.

Lowry (1997) suggests problems may occur if there are personality clashes between the parties involved. This may be resolved if there is more than one mentor available. Mentors have identified time limitation as a disadvantage of contracts, compared with other teaching strategies, especially when first implemented (McAllister, 1996). This may be caused by the learners being unaccustomed to taking an active role in their learning, and therefore needing additional support from their mentor, and the mentors' unfamiliarity with this role.

Conclusions

By promoting a sense of ownership, learning contracts provide a means of encouraging learners to take responsibility for their own professional development. Implementing learning contracts may be a new skill for learners, hence support may be necessary when they are initially introduced. Similarly, mentors who are unfamiliar to the process may benefit from attending relevant workshops.

The flexibility of learning contracts, which are used at any stage of a learner's professional career and in a variety of learning environments, enable them to be considered as a valuable tool in CPD.

Acknowledgements

The author would like to thank all those who participated in the workshops on learning contracts at the CPD conference and the fieldwork educators' conference, and Nicola Spalding and Chia Swee Hong, Lecturers in Occupational Therapy, University of East Anglia, for their useful comments. Figure 8.1 is redrawn with kind permission of the School of Occupational Therapy and Physiotherapy, University of East Anglia.

References

Anderson G, Boud D, Sampson J (1996) *Learning Contracts: A Practical Guide.* Kogan Page, London

Brookfield SD (1996) *Understanding and Facilitating Adult Learning.* Open University, Milton Keynes

Cross V (1996) Introducing learning contracts into physiotherapy clinical education. *Physiotherapy* **82**(1): 21–7

Dart B, Clarke J (1991) Helping students become better learners: a case study in teacher education. *Higher Educ* **22**: 317–35

Donald JG (1976) *Contracting for Learning.* Centre for Learning and Development, McGill University, Montreal

Knowles MS (1990) *The Adult Learner: A Neglected Species.* 4th edn. Gulf Publishing, Houston, Texas

Lowry M (1997) Using learning contracts in clinical practice. *Prof Nurse* **12**(4): 280–3

Martens K (1981) Self-directed learning: an option for nursing education. *Nurs Outlook* **29**: 472–7

Martenson D, Schwab P (1993) Learning by mutual commitment: broadening the concept of learning contracts. *Med Teacher* **15**(1): 11–15

McAllister M (1996) Learning contracts: an Australian experience. *Nurs Educ Today* **16**: 199–205

Quinn FM (1988) *The Principles and Practice of Nurse Education.* 2nd edn. Chapman and Hall, London

Tompkins C, McGraw M-J (1988) The negotiated learning contract. In: Boud D, ed. *Developing Student Autonomy in Learning.* 2nd edn. Kogan Page, London: 172–91

Key points

✿ Learning contracts are derived from the ideas of educators, who believe that what adults choose to learn on their own initiative is learned more deeply and permanently than in 'traditional' education, where the learning process is structured primarily by the teacher and the institution.

✿ Learning contracts encourage self-direction, thus enabling learners to control their learning experiences to meet their own needs and develop skills to educate themselves.

✿ Stages involved in developing a learning contract include: identify a relevant learning need; establish goals or objectives; specify learning resources and strategies; determine the evidence of accomplishment; state how the evidence will be validated, and criteria for assessment; review the contract; carry out the contract; and submission and self-assessment.

✿ Learning contracts take into account individuals' different learning styles and pace of learning, thus increasing motivation.

✿ Implementing learning contracts may be a new skill for learners, hence support may be necessary when they are initially introduced.

✿ Similarly, mentors who are unfamiliar to the process may benefit from attending relevant workshops.

✿ The flexibility of learning contracts enable them to play an important role in professional development portfolios.

9

Fieldwork education as evidence of continuing professional development

Catherine Wells, Hilary Lawler

This chapter highlights fieldwork education as a forum for collecting evidence of professional growth. Methods of collecting evidence are suggested to enable occupational therapists and physiotherapists involved in the clinical supervision of students to develop their professional development portfolios. It also seeks to address the question of how qualified therapists can use this supervisory experience to provide evidence of their own continuing professional development (CPD), thus increasing their skills and raising the whole profile of this important part of the course curriculum.

Introduction

Continuing professional development (CPD) is essential for all occupational therapists and physiotherapists. Stephenson (1998) states 'it is not an option' if therapists are to abide by their profession's code of conduct. CPD can be achieved not only by attending courses on areas of clinical interest, thus increasing clinical competence, but also by using the tools outlined in previous chapters in this book.

Fieldwork education provides an alternative forum for CPD, as all aspects of it impact on the educational process that leads the student to gaining state registration. To ensure that the experience remains innovative, informative and challenging, while paying attention to achieving competence for fitness to practice, student and fieldwork educator, manager and faculty should have confidence in a system that encourages both personal and professional development.

Fieldwork education is an important aspect of any degree course in occupational therapy and physiotherapy. As it occupies one-third of the curriculum, the fieldwork educator (clinical supervisor) plays a significant part in ensuring that the student has a role model committed to developing professional expertise.

This chapter seeks to address the question of how qualified therapists can use this supervisory experience to provide evidence of their own CPD, thus increasing their skills and raising the whole profile of this important part of the course curriculum.

Factors affecting fieldwork education

The provision of high-quality fieldwork education remains a statutory requirement for gaining a license to practice. However, there are a number of factors that impact on its provision:

- Little specific funding is available for the equivalent of one year of a three-year BSc (Hons) course curriculum
- There is an expectation of clinicians to take a constant stream of students, from different academic years, different time scales and with different levels of preparation

- Removal of the payments to fieldwork educators (EL95/96; Department of Health, 1995) was a controversial decision, resulting in some trusts paying the supervisor's allowance, while others consider that this aspect of the job falls within the profession's code of conduct (College of Occupational Therapists, 1995; Chartered Society of Physiotherapy, 1996) and therefore should be perceived as part of the job description
- Recent changes in health and social care policy, eg. the NHS and Community Care Act 1990, have led to increased competition that has resulted in huge pressures on workloads and the throughput of patients
- Clinical practice has altered with the move to community care, resulting in space and time needing to be used more creatively to enable the student to gain appropriate experience. This places an increasing demand on the fieldwork educator to facilitate a quality placement, which may lead to a reluctance by community therapists to have students
- Assessment of clinical practice is undertaken outside the academic environment across a wide range of clinical specialties. This process gives the fieldwork educators an opportunity to make explicit the knowledge, skills and attitudes that are inherent within their practice, and to use it as a contributory tool for providing evidence of CPD.

Linking CPD to fieldwork

A fieldwork educator's course might be one of the early pieces of evidence obtained to demonstrate CPD in clinical supervision. The course provides the opportunity to explore the expectations and responsibilities of those involved in the clinical experience: the school, the student and the fieldwork educator.

As therapists it is possible to reflect on our experiences and identify critical incidents or periods of time during which it is possible to say that some kind of learning experience has occurred, and this forms part of our personal or professional growth. Taking responsibility for supervising a student could be identified as such an experience.

Stengelhofen (1993) defines the role of the fieldwork educator as:

- Managing the work experience provision
- Facilitating learning
- Extending knowledge and promoting its application
- Promoting skill development
- Promoting professionalism.

This process offers the opportunity for professional development, as it demands change and growth in both parties.

Alsop and Ryan (1996) pursue the role further and cite the following as aspects of professional growth:

- Professional competence and confidence
- The ability to evaluate your own professional skills, behaviour and performance.

Figure 9.1 provides a starting point for considering the impact that the various tools of CPD have on fieldwork education. These tools formed the basis of the workshops held at the CPD conference at the University of East Anglia in 1997. Each topic is being explored in the series of chapters within this book.

In order to use fieldwork education in this way it is necessary to explain some of the tools identified within the diagram in further detail.

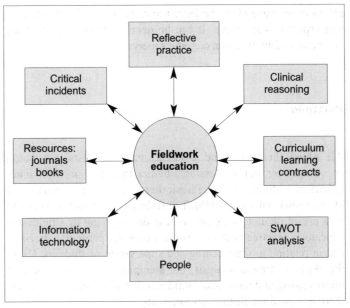

Figure 9.1. Impact of tools of CPD on fieldwork education. (SWOT=strengths, weaknesses, opportunities and threats.)

SWOT analysis

A SWOT (strengths, weaknesses, opportunities and threats) analysis can provide a focus for reflection and discussion for clinical educators. It can be used by the novice fieldwork educator as a means of highlighting any areas within a therapist's own performance that need attention before taking on the task of student supervision. It is also a tool that can be used by experienced fieldwork educators as a means of reviewing their performance and ensuring development in that aspect of their work. It can be done alone or as part of the appraisal system or within ongoing supervision.

Portfolio

All physiotherapists and occupational therapists are being encouraged by their professional bodies to keep a portfolio/diary (Chartered Society of Physiotherapy, 1996; College of Occupational Therapy, 1995). The reflective diary component can be a useful method of demonstrating development in a fieldwork educator's practice both in terms of his or her particular specialty and in relation to the teaching and supervision of students. Using the skills of critical analysis, the therapist can identify areas of improvement and increased confidence as well as situations where there is a need for further development.

Critical incident analysis

Critical incidents are likely to occur during the course of student supervision. These enable a learning experience for both student and clinical educator through reflection upon the incident both individually and together, thus providing an opportunity for personal and professional growth.

As highlighted earlier, Alsop and Ryan (1996) regard 'evaluation of professional skills, behaviour and performance' as an important aspect of development. The learning contract provides a vehicle for this. The student will be working towards identifiable goals, with the fieldwork educator using his or her skills to facilitate the learning or skill acquisition, thus enabling a two-way process.

Evidence of supervision of students can be included in the professional development portfolio. Feedback on the process of supervision is obtainable from students, peers and the educational establishment. The ability to provide constructive feedback in turn enhances the development of others, ensuring that the process of examining and explaining performance becomes almost automatic. This process demands commitment and the ability to look critically at one's self. However, it may not always seem possible to find sufficient time to do this adequately.

Conclusions

Evidence of CPD through fieldwork education may begin with attendance at a fieldwork educator's course, at basic and advanced levels, but then goes beyond this to encompass and demonstrate the unique role that supervising a student plays in achieving CPD. As with all aspects of CPD this could be a paper exercise, or it could be an opportunity to really demonstrate the development of skills and to enhance the credibility of fieldwork education. Therefore, CPD is a method of assuring quality, not only in current professionals but also in students, who will become the professionals of the future.

References

Alsop A, Ryan S (1996) *Making the Most of Fieldwork Education: A Practical Approach*. Chapman and Hall, London

Chartered Society of Physiotherapy (1996) *Rules of Professional Conduct*. Chartered Society of Physiotherapy, London

College of Occupational Therapists (1995) *Code of Ethics and Professional Conduct for Occupational Therapists*. College of Occupational Therapists, London

Department of Health (1995) *Non-Medical Education and Training: Planning for 1996/7 Education (Commissioning (EL(95)96)*. NHS Executive, Leeds

Key points

- ⌘ Fieldwork education provides a forum for personal and professional development.
- ⌘ The tools of reflective practice can be used to demonstrate evidence from the supervisory process.
- ⌘ Evidence of CPD through fieldwork education may begin with attendance at a fieldwork educator's course, at basic and advanced levels, but then goes beyond this to encompass and demonstrate the unique role that supervising a student plays in achieving CPD.

10

Linking registration to the demonstration of continued competence

Peter Burley

From July–September 2002 the Health Professions Council (HPC) consulted on how it should approach continuing professional development (CPD) and the related functions of continued and re-registration. A number of strategic decisions emerged. However, the Health Professions Order did not give the HPC the statutory authority for a 'revalidation' scheme, as developed by the General Medical Council. Revalidation is about securing continued satisfactory performance through peer and lay review. The scheme will be incremental and start with consultants in the NHS who can integrate it with their annual appraisals.

Introduction

In 2000 the government was concerned that the public had lost confidence in health professions. However, it went on to say that health professions' standing could be restored if they, among other remedies, could demonstrate their members' continued competence through some statutory scheme.

When JM Consulting Ltd (1996) had looked at these assertions on behalf of the government at an earlier date, they identified the failure to link continued registration to continued competence as one of the major flaws in the power of the Council for Professions Supplementary to Medicine. The government accepted this in the 1999 Health Act.

State registration modernized

After a period of consultation and debate, from August 2000–February 2002, the government enacted the Health Professions Order (HPO) to modernize state registration for the 12 professions regulated by the then Council for Professions Supplementary to Medicine. The HPO created the Health Professions Council (HPC) from 1 April 2002, with a brief explicitly including competence and continuing professional development (CPD).

CPD is currently the responsibility of the 12 professional bodies regulated by the HPC. Partly in recognition of this, the Allied Health Professions were awarded a contract in 2002 by the Department of Health to make recommendations on 'demonstrating continued competence through CPD'. The Allied Health Professions project will map and analyse the territory and options in CPD; it is known that the project is looking at a work-based approach, rather than at an academic, qualifications-based approach.

From July–September 2002 the HPC consulted on how it should approach CPD and the related functions of continued and re-registration. Over 8000 responses were received; a great many were on these specific topics and expressed concern that registration could be made too onerous. A number of strategic decisions emerged from this process, including:

- The function of ensuring continued competence is linked to conduct and registration powers in the HPO, and not to CPD powers
- A CPD scheme would be consulted on separately, and would not commence until 2006
- The HPC would seek to work with the professional bodies rather than to duplicate or supplant their work.

It also emerged that the HPO did not give the HPC the statutory authority for a 'revalidation' scheme, as developed by the General Medical Council (GMC) (see below).

CPD schemes

For some background and perspective, the two largest current health CPD schemes are the post-registration education programme (PREP) for nurses, midwives and health visitors, and continuing medical education (CME) for doctors. PREP works through self-assessment of needs and self-certification of having met those needs every three years. This generates around 250 000 PREP portfolios each year. CME works through prior accreditation of the quality and relevance of self-directed education by the medical royal colleges, and then through doctors' self-certification of attendance at these colleges. PREP's great weakness is that most nurses' submissions will never be scrutinized; CME makes no direct link with doctors' performance. PREP, however, is evolving and being reviewed, particularly in terms of remedial and corrective measures, and CME will be complemented with 'revalidation' by the GMC.

Revalidation scheme

The GMC has obtained the statutory authority for a revalidation scheme for all doctors, which was finalized in May 2001 after widespread consultation (GMC, 2000). Revalidation is about securing continued satisfactory performance through peer and lay review. It encompasses elements of the supervision processes of psychotherapeutic and other professions, of management appraisal of staff and of CPD. Each doctor will have to keep a comprehensive professional log and be scrutinized by two colleagues and one lay person every 5 years. There will be extensive remedial and corrective provision at the GMC. The scheme will be incremental and start with consultants in the NHS who can integrate it with their annual appraisals.

Helpful developments

The HPC needs to devise a scheme whereby therapists can be supported and developed, rather than overwhelmed, by the need to demonstrate continued competence. Some helpful developments are already emerging (and being looked at by the Allied Health Professions project):

- Linking demonstration of competence to existing processes, eg. staff appraisal or professional supervision
- Building on the pre-registration preparation and support for lifelong learning that all recently trained therapists will have gained
- Using all available information technology support and resources

- Linking demonstration of competence to the therapist's own sense of professional identity and pride.

Demonstration of continued competence is the challenge and the defining issue for all professions. To be sustainable, it needs to be realistic and to be its own reward and satisfaction.

References

Department of Health (2000) *Modernising Regulation — the New Health Professions Council*. Stationery Office, London

General Medical Council (2000) *Revalidating Doctors — Ensuring Standards, Securing the Future*. GMC, London

JM Consulting Ltd (1996) *The Regulation of Health Professions*. JM Consulting Ltd, Bristol

Key points

❧ CPD is currently the responsibility of the 12 professional bodies regulated by the Health Professions Council.

❧ The General Medical Council has obtained the statutory authority for a revalidation scheme for all doctors.

❧ Each doctor will have to keep a comprehensive professional log and be scrutinized by two colleagues and one lay person every 5 years.

❧ Demonstration of continued competence is the challenge and the defining issue for all professions.

11

Stakeholder perspectives on continuing professional development

Eve Pringle, Ann Moore

This chapter describes the findings from the Kent and Sussex education consortia project for post-registration education of professions allied to medicine and clinical psychology. Adopting a stakeholder approach, it explores the different perspectives of key stakeholders and makes recommendations that inform the development of a continuing professional development (CPD) framework.

Introduction

The Kent and Sussex education consortia project for post-registration education of professions allied to medicine (PAMs) and clinical psychology aimed to explore the continuing professional development (CPD) needs of PAMs and clinical psychology within a rapidly changing policy context (Pringle, 1999, 2000).

Recent changes affecting professional regulation and funding for CPD, including the introduction of the Health Professions Council (HPC) and the creation of workforce development confederations (which will replace local education consortia early next year), have highlighted the need for a coordinated CPD PAMs strategy to replace former *ad hoc* arrangements (Department of Health, 2000a,b).

Education and training can also be found at the heart of the Department of Health's recently published strategy for the allied health professions (Department of Health, 2000c). Local stakeholders responsible for CPD therefore need to consider how best they can meet the demand for both effective and cost-effective CPD initiatives.

This project developed a stakeholder approach to CPD, based on qualitative data gathered from practitioners, professional and senior NHS managers, higher education providers and representatives from within the Kent and Sussex education consortia.

Method

The project ran from April 1999–July 2000 (Pringle, 1999, 2000). A qualitative approach was adopted in order to explore the attitudes and perceptions of the key CPD stakeholders and to examine how organizational processes and structures (eg. appraisal), designed to support CPD within the NHS, work in practice.

Case studies were conducted in two joint acute and community NHS trusts within the Kent and Sussex education consortia boundaries. Within the trusts, seven in-depth interviews were carried out with a sample of general managers with responsibility for CPD. Thirteen in-depth interviews were conducted with professional heads of department from occupational therapy, physiotherapy, chiropody, radiography, speech and language therapy, dietetics and clinical psychology.

Eleven focus groups were arranged in the two sites: 63 practitioners from the separate professional groups participated in the focus groups. Contact was made with representatives from the professional associations, and a national network of interested managers, educators and practitioners was established following the publication of a letter in the relevant professional journals, which invited interest in the project.

The focus group and individual interview tapes were transcribed *verbatim*. The analysis used an iterative approach, ie. transcripts were read repeatedly in order to identify common themes (Glaser and Strauss, 1967; Morgan, 1993). The key themes, outlined below, form the basis for the development of a framework.

Appraisal

Appraisal of NHS staff has become more widespread following the introduction of quality standards into the service (Service First Unit, 1999). Over half of the practitioners in the focus groups had been appraised, in line with the government's requirement that appraisal systems are established for all professional staff in the NHS by April 2000 (Department of Health, 1999). Unfilled senior posts were cited as being responsible for the absence of appraisal in some departments, resulting in interruption of the 'cascading down' process. In other cases, reorganization was given as the reason why appraisal systems had not been put in place:

> *'We were supposed to introduce appraisal, but there were a thousand other things to do. Do we move services to a new site or do we introduce appraisal? Well it's a fairly obvious answer' (Radiography manager).*

The case study site in which a merger had recently occurred provided an example of how education and training were often the first 'casualty' of reorganization (Devlin, 1999).

Both practitioners and managers were critical of the appraisal system introduced as a part of 'Investors in people', the national standard relating employee development to organizational goals and performance. They described the system as unnecessarily bureaucratic. The quality of appraisal appeared to vary considerably, with some practitioners recounting that it amounted to little more than a 'chat'. For others, it was a more structured and positive experience:

> *'It made me stop and think about what I had achieved, what I had been doing and where I might want to go'* *(Practitioner focus group).*

Ideally, appraisal should involve preparation from both the manager and the individual before a formal meeting (Mayo, 1998). Comments made during the focus groups suggested that practitioners did not prepare formally for appraisal, seeing this as the line manager's responsibility. Tools already exist that could help practitioners make more use of appraisal, such as the use of critical incidents, surveys, risk assessment, patient complaints and reflective diaries (Grant and Stanton, 1998). However, there was little evidence that these were either widely understood or used in practice. Practitioners, particularly those trained some time ago, appeared to need support in how to approach CPD, and guidance in the use of needs assessment techniques.

Several of the professional managers suggested that they too would have valued more guidance and support concerning their role in appraisal. They felt that their own training needs were often overlooked:

> *'So long as I do my job of running the service, people [senior management] are actually very complacent' (Occupational therapy manager).*

The findings suggested that there needs to be greater appreciation by all stakeholders of the importance of appraisal. The roles and responsibilities of all those involved need to be clarified at an organizational level in an attempt to make it a genuine starting point for CPD rather than a bureaucratic exercise, carried out to keep the 'Investors in people' sign outside the building.

Portfolios

Fifty-nine percent (*n*=63) of those participating in the focus groups said that they owned a professional log or portfolio. However, few practitioners were actually using their portfolios as an aid to 'reflective' practice (Schön, 1987). Reasons given were that portfolios were poorly designed, there was insufficient time and that little guidance had been provided to assist practitioners in 'getting started' with portfolios:

> *'I was just handed one and said "there you go" — I hadn't even been talked through it' (Practitioner focus group).*

Practitioners who had been working for many years found the task of starting a portfolio daunting. There were many other unresolved issues surrounding portfolios, which emerged during discussions in the focus groups.

For example:

- What was the portfolio's role within appraisal?
- If portfolios are to be used in appraisal, should practitioners be allocated work time to complete them?
- To what extent can portfolios fulfil their role as personal documents if they are scrutinized by managers?

Portfolios are likely to become a key component in any mandatory system of CPD, providing a cost-effective, convenient and individual record of learning, based on reflective practice.

There was a lack of clear consensus regarding the role of portfolios within appraisal, and there needs to be discussion leading to the development of clear guidelines. Higher education has a responsibility to ensure that newly qualified practitioners understand the role of portfolios, and that they are equipped with the skills to maintain them on entering practice. A comment from a manager suggested that this is not always the case at present:

> '*The juniors coming out of college appear to be viewing their portfolios as a folder that they put their certificate of attendance in*' (Occupational therapy manager).

Higher education could also be providing post-registration guidance for practitioners and managers on developing the skills necessary to use portfolios as an effective form of CPD. Those responsible within higher education for delivering a CPD programme, although willing to collaborate, felt that they were constrained by limited resources, particularly lack of time and the skills necessary to deliver tailor-made, work-based programmes.

Work-based opportunities

There was an imbalance between the provision of opportunities for work-based CPD, compared with external courses in the case-study sites. Attending external courses and conferences was the main source of CPD for most practitioners and managers. The literature suggests that work-based learning is both effective and cost-effective (Grant and Stanton, 1998). Despite this, work-based education tended to be viewed as limited to the 'latest computer course'. Practitioners whose personal circumstances made it difficult for them to attend courses away from home were keen for more work-based opportunities to be developed.

This begs the question as to why work-based opportunities, including portfolio workshops, mentoring and peer supervisory structures and initiatives, such as journal clubs, were not more in evidence? A possible explanation was the way in which training projections and budget allocations were made within the trusts, which created an incentive for managers to use budgets for 'away training'. Managers were often in the position of having to spend money quickly or face losing it, and this did not support longer-term or innovative planning. Managers and practitioners were also in the habit of thinking about education and training in terms of external courses, and the pressure on managers meant that there was little opportunity for them to be creative:

> *'You are in a situation where people are just surviving. You can only really plan CPD when you are confident and you can see a way ahead' (Speech and language therapy manager).*

Higher education providers expressed an interest in developing work-based learning in collaboration with service providers, and there were a few examples where this had taken place. However, they acknowledged that more could have been achieved, especially with regard to the accreditation of work-based learning.

One participant felt that at present there was a lot of rhetoric surrounding 'partnerships' between higher education and service providers and that, in reality:

> *'...some managers just want to send their staff on courses and for them to come back ready for work' (Higher education focus group).*

Shared learning

The government is committed to promoting shared learning, possibly because there is an assumption that it will assist in breaking down 'barriers' between the professions (Hopkins *et al*, 1996). The findings from the project suggest that there needs to be some caution exercised concerning the balance between uni-professional and shared learning. The case studies highlighted that practitioners were working in increasingly specialist areas, and their CPD needs were often linked directly to their specialism. Practitioners felt that shared learning, at a post-registration level, should complement not replace specialist professional education and training.

Few shared initiatives for CPD existed, suggesting that there was room for development in this area. One possible reason for the lack of shared initiatives could have been the fact that PAMs forums in trusts were difficult to establish. Problems of communication between the separate professions, struggles over how they represent one another at board level and the challenge of maintaining continuity in an ever-changing NHS limited their effectiveness. As a consequence, PAMs were limited in their ability to collaborate with one another and in their ability to influence decision-making at a strategic level:

> *'We did have a forum where we met as PAMs, but it seems to have gone by the wayside. It was supposed to have been our link with the board' (Occupational therapy manager).*

Local shared learning initiatives may be more likely to emerge if these PAMs forums become established and the separate professions recognize their joint agenda, adopting a 'strength in numbers' approach to lobbying for resources and funding.

Bringing about a culture change that will support both shared and work-based CPD presents a challenge. If shared learning and work-based CPD initiatives are to be successfully integrated at a practice level, similar strategies to those used to promote evidence-based practice, aimed at changing attitudes, need to be considered (Dunning *et al*, 1998). Managers crucially need to be allowed the time to develop longer-term strategic plans for training and development. Additionally, they need to be offered practical assistance, in the form of a CPD facilitator, in how to approach the task of developing accredited work-based and shared opportunities for practitioners. Funding and budgetary arrangements within trusts would need to be more creatively allocated in order to provide incentives for managers to develop such initiatives.

Evaluating CPD and making use of 'new' knowledge and skills

Both the trusts involved in the project had attempted to put in place CPD evaluation systems. However, these focused on the quantifiable aspects of time and costs associated with CPD, and an assessment of the impact on practitioner's effectiveness or benefits to patient care had not been attempted:

> *'The actual evaluation was very general....it amounted to how many training days we had related to how much we spent, and it did sound good and cheap' (Occupational therapy manager).*

The literature indicates that the successful integration of new knowledge depends on it being reinforced in the clinical setting (Grant and Stanton, 1998). The findings from this study, however, suggest that many practitioners felt that there was little opportunity for them to apply new skill and ability:

> *'It's a waste of time if we spend time learning something and then don't use it to its full potential' (Radiography focus group).*

This appeared to be a specific problem for practitioners who had worked towards a higher degree. Many of them were frustrated by the fact that although they gained personal satisfaction, their work had not changed to accommodate their new skills. A few of the managers interviewed simply did not see a MSc as a useful form of CPD. One manager stated that there was little point in sending a practitioner on a MSc course because 'it was of no value to the trust' and of little value to the individual because 'we are not going to promote them' (Radiography manager).

From a general management perspective, however, the frustration that some practitioners experienced was the result of the failure to match professional needs to the wider business plan of the trust. Few practitioners were familiar with the business plan, describing it as a 'public relations exercise'. Professional managers influenced the way in which practitioners perceived the organization in which they worked, and it appeared that it was down to the skills of the individual professional manager to translate the business plan into meaningful, tangible learning goals for practitioners.

Communication and collaboration between stakeholders

Barriers in communication and collaboration between the separate professions can be explained partly as emanating from the era of inter- and intra-trust competition pursued by the former Conservative Government (Department of Health, 1989). There was little evidence of the new spirit of partnership and collaboration, despite rhetoric to this effect (Department of Health, 1998). The separate professions found it difficult to grasp the opportunities of 'working together' for a shared aim, possibly because they lacked the necessary skills (Alter and Jerald, 1993). A lack of understanding among stakeholders about the education consortia contributed to confusion about their role in CPD.

Each trust was responsible for developing CPD initiatives under the requirements of clinical governance, but the commitment to creating an overall strategic vision at the level of the consortia had not been grasped. Higher education representatives felt that the consortia could assume more of a coordinating role:

> *'It would have been sensible if there could be one person who could be responsible for channelling the CPD needs [of the consortia] through us'* (Higher education provider).

Some participants argued that the PAMs had been thrown together organizationally simply because 'we are not nurses and were not doctors' (Dietician manager). Others indicated that the PAMs were beginning to develop a shared agenda. The strategic planning of CPD among the PAMs professions and between separate provider units was an, as yet, uncharted area offering enormous potential for the future commissioning of higher education. The publication of the Department of Health's strategy (Department of Health, 2000a) may act to stimulate such developments. Establishing a policy on CPD within the confederation would have an immediate benefit in assisting higher education providers in developing courses or facilitator-based workplace initiatives that meet the needs of several provider units.

Conclusions

What clearly emerged from analysis of the data was the need to ensure that the foundations necessary for CPD were in place. Practitioners working in departments that are inadequately staffed will not prioritize CPD. Similarly, if appraisal systems are poor, CPD needs will not be identified. Therefore, practitioners need to be supported by adequate workforce planning, a professional manager skilled in staff development and an effective appraisal scheme.

The project also demonstrated the importance, particularly in the current climate of partnership working, of approaching CPD from a joint stakeholder perspective. Widespread enthusiasm and support for CPD exists, but in order to harness this, the separate professions and key stakeholders need to collaborate. An opportunity for a constructive way forward is present as non-medical education and training funds become available to PAMs, and the government recognizes the important role that PAMs play in delivering the NHS Plan (Department of Health, 2000c).

Acknowledgements

The authors would like to acknowledge the support of both the Kent and Sussex education consortia. Grateful thanks to all those individuals who participated in and contributed to PAMs post-registration education project.

References

Alter C, Jerald H (1993) *Organizations Working Together*. Sage, London
Department of Health (1989) *Working for Patients*. HMSO, London
Department of Health (1998) *The New NHS: Modern, Dependable*. HMSO, London
Department of Health (1999) *Continuing Professional Development: Quality in the New NHS*. HMSO, London
Department of Health (2000a) *Modernising Regulation – The New Health Professions Council*. Department of Health, London

Department of Health (2000b) *A Health Service of all the Talents: Developing the NHS Workforce. A Consultation Document on the Review of Workforce Planning.* HMSO, London

Department of Health (2000c) *Meeting the Challenge: A Strategy for the Allied Health Professionals.* NHS Executive, London

Devlin M (1999) States of flux. *Health Serv J* **6 May**: 24–5

Dunning M, Abi-Aad G, Gilbert D, Gillam S, Livett H (1998) *Turning Evidence into Everyday Practice.* The Falmer Press, London

Grant J, Stanton F (1998) *The Effectiveness of Continuing Professional Development — A Report for the Chief Medical Officer's Review of CPD in Practice.* Joint Centre for Education in Medicine, London

Glaser B, Strauss A (1967) *The Discovery of Grounded Theory.* Aldine Publishing, Chicago

Hopkins A, Solomon J, Abelson J (1996) Shifting boundaries in professional care. *J Roy Soc Med* **89**: 364–71

Mayo A (1998) *Developing a Training and Development Strategy.* Institute of Personnel and Development, London

Morgan D (1993) *Successful Focus Groups: Advancing the State of the Art.* Sage, London

Pringle E (1999) Post-registration education: exploring the issues for PAMs. *Br J Ther Rehabil* **6**(12): 591–4

Pringle E (2000) *Pushing an Open Door — A Stakeholder Approach to Developing CPD Initiatives for PAMs and Clinical Psychology.* The Research Centre for Health Professions, University of Brighton, Brighton

Service First Unit (1999) *A Guide to Quality Schemes for the Public Sector.* Cabinet Office, London

Schön D (1987) *Educating the Reflective Practitioner: Towards a New Design for Teaching and Learning in the Professions.* Josey Bass, San Francisco

Key points

The Kent and Sussex education consortia project for post-registration education of professions allied to medicine (PAMs) and clinical psychology identified the following areas of priorities:

⌘ In order for practitioners to engage in CPD, they need to be supported by adequate workforce planning, a professional manager skilled in staff development and an effective appraisal scheme.

⌘ More work-based and shared learning opportunities in CPD need to be established for PAMs.

⌘ Representation of PAMs and clinical psychologists at a senior level within trusts and workforce confederations is necessary in order to highlight the specific CPD needs of these professions.

⌘ Closer collaboration needs to occur between the separate professions and the separate stakeholders in developing a shared CPD agenda.

12

Understanding reflective practice in occupational therapy

Gail Boniface

Reflection has been seen in a number of professions allied to medicine, nursing and teaching as a necessary prerequisite for the development of appropriately evaluated practice. This chapter identifies occupational therapists' understanding of reflective practice in three separate settings: mental health, stroke rehabilitation and general medicine. The factors that encourage or hinder reflection are investigated and analysed to inform future practice.

Introduction

Reflection has been seen in a number of professions allied to medicine (Crabtree and Lyons, 1997), nursing (Johns, 1994) and teaching (Reed *et al*, 2002) as a necessary prerequisite for the development of appropriately evaluated practice.

This chapter describes a study undertaken as a collaborative inquiry into occupational therapists' views of the nature of their reflective practice, and their understanding of reflection itself.

Reflection

Schön (1983) views reflection as the way in which the individual professional develops a repertoire of knowledge and ability, which can be drawn upon in future situations. It is also the way in which otherwise unobservable thinking, leading to action, is brought into the public domain. As Meyers (1986) describes it, identifying reflection is a way of 'making implicit thought processes explicit'.

Superficial reflection

Reflection can be viewed in a number of ways: as a way of thinking (Dewey, 1933); as natural evolution of humans (Habermas, 1971); as a structure for action (Mezirow, 1981; Fish and Twinn, 1997) and as an evaluation tool. However, when used for evaluating the therapist's work, reflection can tend to stop at a somewhat superficial level. Such superficial reflection leads to an evaluation of a therapist's practice and work, without leading the therapist to evaluate him or herself as a therapist.

This was noted by Richardson and Maltby (1995), who analysed the reflective diaries of student nurses in relation to a scale they developed based on Mezirow's (1981) seven levels of reflectivity. These levels of reflectivity begin with an awareness or description of reflection, and lead up to a more conceptual level of theoretical reflectivity. Richardson and Maltby's findings from the diaries showed that the student nurses had a tendency to reflect at the more superficial, descriptive level; while the level at which reflection led to a change in perspective, or even belief system, was avoided.

Models of reflection

A number of models of reflection (Mezirow, 1981; Kolb, 1984; Boud *et al*, 1985; Johns, 1994; Fish and Twinn, 1997) are available to those wishing to structure their reflection. They all start from the position of describing the experience that is to be reflected upon. The models also describe the need for reflection to start from the identification of a problem. Ways of dealing with the problem are devised, tested and then evaluated. This reflective cycle has similarities with problem-solving. What differentiates reflection from problem-solving is that part of the potential solution is the therapist developing a new view of him or herself, or a confirmation of his or her existing view.

Table 12.1 summarizes the stages of reflection and their level of complexity, common to most models.

Table 12.1. Stages of reflection (based on various models)	
Setting the scene	Lower level of reflection
Telling the story of the event to be reflected upon	Lower level of reflection
Identifying critical occurrences	Lower level of reflection
Linking the story and critical occurrences to previous events or knowledge	Middle level of reflection
Identifying feelings associated with the story or critical occurrences	Middle level of reflection
Identifying and challenging blindspots associated with those feelings, such as prejudices	Middle level of reflection
Identifying what has been learnt from reflection	Middle level of reflection
Deciding whether a change is now necessary as a result of the reflection	Middle level of reflection
Identifying and critiquing the belief system upon which our actions are based	High level of reflection (reflecting on reflections)
Taken from Mezirow (1981), Schön (1983), and Fish and Twinn (1997)	

Criticism of models of reflection

Models of reflection are criticized by Clarke *et al* (1996), who are particularly concerned that the structuring of reflection runs the danger of creating a technical, rational model of reflection. Such a model of reflection can be encouraged by the ways in which structuring is used. For example, diaries have been identified as leading to superficial reflection (Foster and Greenwood, 1998).

Barnett (1997) urges us to be suspicious of the organization's keenness on reflection leading to its desired goal of increased effectiveness, rather than the growth of the professional.

Aims of the inquiry

Schön (1983) describes professional action as intuitive and, consequently, difficult to explain. Therefore, it becomes almost impossible for the outsider to identify how the professional decides to act, if that professional cannot articulate that process for him or herself.

The collaborative inquiry aimed to articulate reflection in the participants' professional practice, through reflection on that practice. In Argyris and Schön's (1974) terms, the participants attempted to name and frame their reflection.

In order to do that, the participants devised the following research questions:

1. What do occupational therapists understand by 'reflection'?
2. What encourages and what hinders that reflection?

Methodology

The participants

It was possible that different therapists in different settings viewed and used reflection differently. Therefore, the nature of reflection was investigated in different settings: hospital, physical and mental health settings. Three separate groups of occupational therapists were recruited into the study:

- Group one: five members, all working in an acute physical setting (ie. general medicine)
- Group two: five members, all working in stroke rehabilitation
- Group three: sixteen members, all working in mental health.

The groups were open and tended to retain a consistent core group of five people throughout the one-year study. The level of the participants' experience was varied, as was their length of employment in their respective workplaces. The reasons for their inclusion in the groups were that they were interested in the subject of reflection and were willing to participate in a collaborative inquiry. Groups one and three included the departmental manager.

It was felt appropriate to investigate the views and experiences of the groups' reflections in diverse settings, but no comparison between groups was intended. Therefore, the groups did not need to be homogenous. The research also intended to identify occupational therapists' views of the issue of reflection. There was no intention to generalize results, rather to use them to inform views of reflection. Thus, the participation in a group was a result of self-selection and was not controlled by the researcher.

The researcher's role was one of participant and facilitator. The ethical and methodological implications of this researcher role are discussed by Heron (1996) as necessitating the taking on and identification of different roles with the groups at different stages in their history as groups. These implications are also considered below in relation to validity issues.

Appropriate research methods

Inquiry methods appropriate to the study of reflection need to be those that actually encourage what is being investigated, ie. reflection. Carr and Kemmis (1983) discuss practice and praxis, describing praxis as something that emerges as a result of reflecting on the carrying out of professional action (practice) in order to improve it. Praxis, in their view, evolves from action – providing that action is evaluated. Their description of the development of praxis closely resembles the process of reflection itself. In their view, one appropriate way of developing praxis based on reflection is through action research, a phrase first attributed to Kurt Lewin (1946).

Much of the literature on types of action research (Carr and Kemmis, 1983; Reason, 1994; Heron, 1996; Bray *et al*, 2000) views the research as that which is carried out with, rather than on, the participants. This seemed to ideally suit the topic of reflection, as Reason's (1994) view that participatory action research is illuminating, soul-bearing and potentially embarrassing is strongly reminiscent of the nature of reflection itself. A collaborative inquiry is also one in which a strong element of reflection is expected.

Collaborative inquiry

Action research, in the form of a collaborative inquiry, emerged as the appropriate methodology for this investigation. There are a number of terms to describe such collaborative approaches, but both Reason (1994) and Bray et al (2000) see similarities between them, where the similarities lie in the amount of reflection required for each approach. The research approach taken was cooperative inquiry which, according to Reason (1988), is 'an essentially emergent process'.

Validity

Heron (1996) describes the validity measures for cooperative inquiry as:
- Research cycling between action and reflection
- A balance between convergence and divergence
- The facilitator taking a falsifying or devil's advocate role
- Authentic group collaboration; occurring as a result of the researcher and the participants recognizing when the researcher was acting as a participant or facilitator.

All of these measures were included in this study, which took place over one year.

Results and discussion

Each of the group's discussions were taped and transcribed. Each transcription was sent to each group member before the next group meeting for comment and checking. Occasionally, this resulted in group members themselves analysing aspects of the data by allocating codes to the raw data and grouping it into categories; a form of indigenous coding by the members (Holstein and Gubrium, 1995).

When carrying out data analysis, Dey (1993) suggests returning to the original research questions to help identify categories in the data. The suggestions for categories inherent in the research questions were 'the nature of reflection' and 'environmental influences on reflection'.

Each transcript was coded line by line, resulting in the raw data being translated into a theoretical description of the issue emerging, which could then be related to the research questions. Consequently, the coded data was sorted to identify similarities, differences and relationships.

For example, the large category of 'environment' emerged from the combination of smaller codes for: supervision, pressure of time; aloneness or togetherness; triggers for reflection; and positive or negative views of occupational therapists. This confirmed that the original research question in relation to 'environments that encourage or hinder reflection' was, in fact, an issue for these occupational therapists.

As a result of this analytical process, the data separated into two distinct elements. The first concerned the process of the inquiry, and the second concerned reflection itself. It is the second issue this chapter now deals with.

Reflection as an innate ability

There was a split between those in the groups who felt reflection was something of which everyone was capable; and those who felt some people were incapable of reflecting.

A group one member seemed to support the innateness of the ability to reflect by saying: 'I think it's intrinsic in a way'. This comment is supported by Habermas' (1971) opinion that reflection is part of human evolution. A member of group two also appeared to support this view, saying:

> *'We wondered if it was more to do with innate personality*
> *issues and that you were an intuitive person able to*
> *reflect, and some people just can't.'*

However, they seemed to contradict themselves by saying 'and some people just can't'. In further contrast, one group two member indicated a total lack of belief in some people's ability to reflect:

> *'I actually think that there are some people who cannot*
> *reflect. I do. I think there are people who have NO insight,*
> *that they drop bombshells and are creating all these*
> *ripples all the way round. They have no idea what it is*
> *that they have done.'*

Yet they went on to indicate that even such inability could possibly be remedied:

> *'I wonder with reflection, if that is something that that*
> *person can be taught or it can be pointed out to them.'*

The idea of the possibility of teaching reflection was eventually agreed upon by other group members and also picked up in other groups. This suggests that the group members felt that in all people there is an innate spark of reflective ability, but this needs to be developed and supported in an appropriate environment.

Reflection as something that can be taught

This general category of teaching and learning reflection grew from the codes of: learning, teaching and encouraging reflection; relevance of reflection; spotting reflection; and assessing reflection in others. The group members felt that students on an occupational therapy course had been selected via a process that considered reflective potential. The group participants also felt that, as professionals who had undergone such a course, they too had reflective potential. The process of the collaborative inquiry demonstrated to them that they needed to develop that potential in both themselves and others. They concluded that reflection could be taught by building on the individual's innate ability to reflect. However, in order to teach reflection, structures (models) that could be internalized needed to be used.

Despite their interest in such structures, the participants were highly critical of some of the ways in which they were used. Reflective diaries were also viewed with suspicion. A group three member said:

> *'I found that with the counselling course that we did, we had to keep a reflective diary, and the reflective diary was taken in and marked as an assignment. And you wrote your diary in such a way that whoever was marking it would know that you were reflective, and most of us made most of it up.'*

This comment is supported by Richardson and Maltby's (1995) view concerning the student nurses' use of reflective diaries:

> *'A number of the students mentioned the assessment of their diary as a barrier to their writing.'*

The views of the group members were that structures of reflection were needed, but that if pre-existing ones were to be used, they had to be used flexibly. Another group three member said:

> *'There are undoubtedly personal structures and there are*
> *formal structures, and I think that you've got to recognize*
> *that personal ones can be very variable and will depend*
> *on each of us and how we go about it.'*

A reflective environment

All group members agreed that reflection can be carried out alone, but is better with someone else. However, there was concern over whether a supervisor was the best person with whom to reflect. This issue highlighted the vulnerability that the researchers felt when they exposed themselves to the openness of reflection, and their reluctance to be open with somebody who was in a management position over them. This is an issue related to whether:

> *'...supervision is a way of controlling, disenfranchising or*
> *pushing (teachers) around, or whether it is an*
> *emancipatory or liberating process' (Smyth, 1985).*

All group members worked in the NHS and identified lack of time as a barrier to reflection. Those in group three felt pressurized to work as care managers as well as occupational therapists. Those in both groups one and two were working as occupational therapists only, but were pressurized to comply with the organization's desire to discharge patients quickly. They felt angry at the lack of organizational time allocated to reflection and CPD. They were also suspicious of an environment that ostensibly valued reflection, yet by its pressures discouraged it.

This is a viewpoint that is supported by Barnett's (1997) previously mentioned suspicion regarding organizations' desire to increase effectiveness rather than promote personal growth of the professional. Environment was thus seen as a potentially major facilitator in the reflective process. But in reality, the environments the participants found themselves in were felt to be inhibitors of that process.

Conclusions and implications for practice

Despite working in different settings, the collaborative group members' understanding and experience of reflection were similar. The following implications for practical use of reflection emerged:

1. Situations where reflection can be identified and recognized need to be devised. This means considering the time needed for reflection. Reflection time may need to be separated out from work actions, especially if the organization does not recognize the need for reflection. However, if reflection is an ongoing circular process, it cannot necessarily be blocked into designated time spaces. It requires the reflector and the organization to recognize this circular nature of reflection and create ideal circumstances for reflection to occur, ie. a reflective working environment

2. Supervision should be split into managerial, professional and personal development supervision, where the challenging and anxiety-inducing reflective element is dealt with outside the managerial remit

3. Reflection can be taught, but there needs to be a spark of ability present. Professional courses need to develop ways of identifying reflective potential in their candidates

4. A safe but challenging environment is necessary for reflection
5. Structures for reflection (models) must be used flexibly to encourage a deeper level of reflection.

References

Argyris C, Schön DA (1974) *Theory in Practice*. Jossey Bass, San Francisco
Barnett R (1997) *Higher Education: A Critical Business*. Oxford Society for Research and Higher Education/Oxford University Press, Milton Keynes
Boud D, Keogh R, Walker D, eds (1985) *Reflection: Turning Experience into Learning*. Kogan Page, London
Bray JN, Lee J, Smith LL, Yorks L (2000) *Collaborative Inquiry in Practice*. Sage, London
Carr W, Kemmis S (1983) *Becoming Critical: Knowing Through Action Research*. Deakin University Printery, Victoria
Clarke B, James C, Kelly J (1996) Reflective practice: reviewing the issues and refocusing the debate. *Intern J Nurs Studies* **33**(2): 171–80
Crabtree M, Lyons M (1997) Focal points and relationships: a study of clinical reasoning. *Br J Occup Ther* **60**(2): 57–64
Dewey J (1933) *How We Think*. Heath and Co, Boston, DC
Dey I (1993) *Qualitative Data Analysis*. Routledge, London
Fish D, Twinn S (1997) *Quality Supervision in the Health Care Professions: Principled Approaches to Practice*. Butterworth-Heinemann, Oxford
Foster J, Greenwood J (1998) Reflection: a challenging innovation for nurses. *Contemp Nurse* **7**(4): 165–72
Habermas J (1971) *Knowledge and Human Interests*. Heinemann, London
Heron J (1996) *Cooperative Inquiry: Research into the Human Condition*. Sage, London
Holstein JA, Gubrium JF (1995) *The Active Interview*. Sage, London
Johns C (1994) Nuances of reflection. *J Clin Nurs* **3**: 71–5
Kolb D (1984) *Experiential Learning as the Science of Learning and Development*. Prentice Hall, New Jersey
Lewin K (1946) Action research and minority problems. *J Soc Issues* **2**: 34–6
Meyers C (1986) *Teaching Students to Think Critically*. Jossey Bass, San Francisco
Mezirow J (1981) A critical theory of adult learning and education. *Adult Educ* **32**(1): 3–24
Reason P, ed (1988) *Human Inquiry in Action*. Sage, London

Reason P, ed (1994) *Participation in Human Inquiry*. Sage, London

Reed Y, Davis H, Nyanabanyaba T (2002) Investigating teachers' 'take-up' of reflective practice from an in-service professional development teacher education programme in South Africa. *Educ Action Res* **10**(2): 253–74

Richardson G, Maltby H (1995) Reflection-on-practice: enhancing student learning. *J Adv Nurs* **22**: 235–42

Schön DA (1983) *The Reflective Practitioner*. Arena, Aldershot

Smyth WJ (1985) Developing a clinical practice of clinical supervision. *J Curr Studies* **17**(1): 1–15

Key points

✳ Despite working in different settings, the collaborative group members' understanding and experience of reflection were similar.

✳ Reflective structures, such as models, should be used flexibly to encourage a deeper level of reflection.

✳ A safe but challenging environment is necessary for reflection.

✳ Reflection can be taught, but there needs to be a spark of ability present. Professional courses need to develop ways of identifying reflective potential in their candidates.

✳ Reflection should lead to challenge or confirmation of belief systems.

✳ The workplace environment can encourage or hamper reflection.